LEARNING TO LEAD

JENNIFER R. NÁJERA

LEARNING TO LEAD

Undocumented Students Mobilizing Education

DUKE UNIVERSITY PRESS
Durham and London
2024

© 2024 DUKE UNIVERSITY PRESS
All rights reserved
Printed in the United States of America on acid-free paper ∞
Project Editor: Michael Trudeau
Designed by A. Mattson Gallagher
Typeset in Minion Pro and Trade Gothic LT Std
by Copperline Book Services

Library of Congress Cataloging-in-Publication Data
Names: Nájera, Jennifer R., [date] author.
Title: Learning to lead : undocumented students mobilizing
education / Jennifer R. Nájera.
Other titles: Undocumented students mobilizing education
Description: Durham : Duke University Press, 2024. |
Includes bibliographical references and index.
Identifiers: LCCN 2024003248 (print)
LCCN 2024003249 (ebook)
ISBN 9781478030539 (paperback)
ISBN 9781478026303 (hardcover)
ISBN 9781478059530 (ebook)
Subjects: LCSH: Noncitizens—Education (Higher)—
California. | College students—Political activity—California.
| Children of immigrants—Education—California. | Student
movements—California.
Classification: LCC LC3746.5.C2 N354 2024 (print) | LCC LC3746.5.C2
(ebook) | DDC 378.1/98109794—DC23/ENG/20240430
LC record available at https://lccn.loc.gov/2024003248
LC ebook record available at https://lccn.loc.gov/2024003249

Cover art: Students with butterfly wings after the Coming Out
of the Shadows event. Photo courtesy of Mafalda Gueta.

To the members of PODER *past, present, and future*

In memory of Joe Najera

And maybe there is no nation of citizenry; they're just territories mapped in place of family, in place of love, the infinite country.

Patricia Engel, *Infinite Country*

Political action on the side of the oppressed must be pedagogical action in the authentic sense of the word.

Paulo Freire, *Pedagogy of the Oppressed*

CONTENTS

ACKNOWLEDGMENTS

This book would not have been possible without the generosity and openness of a group of undocumented young people and allies who welcomed me into their lives—both politically and personally. When working with undocumented people, it's delicate to use people's real names, but I'm especially grateful to the students who were active members of Providing Opportunities, Dreams, and Education in Riverside (PODER) during 2013–16. It's been one of my greatest privileges to have walked alongside these young people during a part of their college years and beyond. They have been some of my greatest teachers, and I am so thankful to them.

I struggled with how to do justice to their stories through my writing; it seemed impossible to capture the family stories, personal journeys, political imperatives, and many emotional highs and lows of living in this country without papers. I am incredibly grateful to Michael Jaime Becerra and Ricky Rodriguez, my brilliant writing group partners. They thoughtfully assessed drafts of every chapter, pushing me to sharper analysis and more creative and nuanced writing.

Special thank-yous go to Ana and Mafalda. I appreciate Ana for being an invaluable adviser, guide, and friend during my research and writing. I'm also very grateful to Mafalda for his openness, generosity, thoughtfulness, and good humor. I've learned so much from you both.

In the middle of this research and writing Laura Enriquez invited me to be part of a research team to examine the effects of immigration policy on undocumented students and students from mixed-status families. Working on that study helped to deepen my understanding of how such policies affect both students and families, regardless of immigration status. Laura, Cecilia Ayón, Annie Ro, and Zulema Valdez were wonderful and insightful colleagues as I grappled with my own book alongside that study.

I would be remiss not to mention the small group of scholars I have come to rely on over the past several years for accountability, advice, and support. Nancy Baker, Charlotte Biltekoff, Carlita Favero, and I first came together through the Faculty Success Program in 2016, and I'm thankful that we've maintained our peer mentorship and friendship now well beyond the program.

To Gisela Fosado at Duke University, thank you for believing in this book, encouraging the writing style, and providing much needed accountability. Thank you also to Alejandra Mejía for helping to shepherd this book to completion.

I'm also grateful to those students who have worked with me on this project over the years with bibliographies and other organizational work: Gemma Aguilar, Morayma Flores Higinio, Rubyd Olvera, and Frank Perez. Every hour of your work helped move this project forward.

When everything began to shut down during March 2020 and I took on the role of department chair shortly thereafter, I relied heavily on the support and encouragement of dear friends to keep this book project moving forward. Tamara Alvarado, Vanessa Alvarado, Keri Castaneda, and Imelda González, thank you for your humor, encouragement, and grace through some very hard moments. Jennifer Escobar, your friendship and support was invaluable to me. And Brenda Sendejo, mi amiga del alma, thank you for always providing the spiritual Chicana feminist perspective I needed. During the last months of reckoning with and writing revisions, Michelle Téllez and Cristina Salinas talked with me about ideas and pushed me to finish the book. Gracias por todo.

To Olga Herrera, Verónica Martínez-Matsuda, and Cristina Salinas, thank you for your steadfast companionship over these past two decades. I'm inspired by your fierce intellect and ability to balance the demands of academia with roles as partners, mothers, sisters, and daughters.

Finally, to my family: my parents, Joe and Rose Najera, laid the foundation for me to be able to do the work that I love. To my partner, Joseph

Sepulveda, thank you for creating the space for me to do fieldwork with the students, for encouraging my writing and providing key moments of accountability, and for always believing in me. To Eliana Rose and Adalia Flor, I hope that someday the stories of these students and families will inspire you to fight and to create the world in which you want to live.

INTRODUCTION

Undocumented Education

Anahí was in seventh grade when Immigration and Customs Enforcement (ICE) agents showed up at her door.[1] Her family shared a house with her aunt and uncle in the southeastern part of the urban sprawl of Los Angeles. Almost every day her parents would leave in the morning to sell tamales and return late in the afternoon. That day they had just returned home to Anahí and her two younger brothers when the agents knocked. A couple of years earlier, Anahí's aunt had petitioned to fix her immigration status. This entailed regular meetings in court, but as the process dragged on, Anahí's aunt eventually stopped going to the appointments. Her aunt knew that the judge could issue an arrest warrant, but after time passed and nothing happened, Anahí's aunt no longer thought much about it. Until the afternoon that ICE agents came to the house. With the warrant, ICE agents—clad in dark bulletproof vests and utility belts—asserted their right to enter and found Anahí's aunt. They handcuffed her, then surveyed the other people in the house. One of the agents turned to Anahí's father and asked him—and she remembers this phrasing—"Are you an illegal?" She recalls that one of the agents spoke Spanish. He was talking directly to her parents, and they understood.

"Eres ilegal?"

Her dad nodded, and the agent handcuffed him.

Then he asked her mom. "Are you an illegal?"

Her mother said yes.

Anahí recalls her younger brothers clinging to their mother. She remembers looking at her father, who was handcuffed, and his dark eyes were fixed on her. She couldn't read his look. She thought it might have something to do with her being the oldest; about knowing what her responsibilities would be if both of her parents were deported. Or maybe he was looking at her and wondering how they would all rebuild their lives in Mexico. Though it was happening in a matter of minutes—seconds—the weight of their collective fear made the moment feel long.

Then something unexpected happened.

The Spanish-speaking ICE agent asked Anahí's mother, "Do you have any US-born children?"

"Yes. My son," she told him, motioning to the one of the young boys whose arms were encircling her body. He looked down at the children as if he were seeing them for the first time.

"Is there anyone who can take care of him?"

"No," Anahí's mother said. "He's little. There's no one who can take care of him."

"OK," the agent told her. "Because you have a US-born son, we're not going to take you."

Anahí's surprise and relief that ICE was not going to arrest her mother turned quickly to a pang of despair as she watched the agents walk her father and her aunt outside, into a white van. She watched it drive away. She would see that van in her mind's eye every time she felt her father's absence. When she felt as if he had abandoned them, she would conjure that image to remind herself that he had not left them. He had been taken.

This moment was one of Anahí's earliest lessons about US immigration policy: this was what it meant to be undocumented—vulnerable, deportable. Immigration and Customs Enforcement was the kind of "police" who could take them away.

Years later, as a student at the University of California (UC), Riverside, Anahí would deepen her understanding of immigration policy in her sociology and Chicano/a studies classes. She learned that ICE was the enforcement arm of the Department of Homeland Security (DHS). She would join an advocacy group for undocumented students on campus called PODER (Providing Opportunities, Dreams, and Education in Riverside). Through PODER she would meet other undocumented students, some of whom had also experienced the deportation of a family member. A father. They were all now part of the UC, a premier public university system that espoused a commitment to supporting its diverse student body, including undocumented students. It was also a system that had appointed Janet Napolitano, the former head of DHS, to its top position the year before Anahí began her freshman year.

In July 2013, when the UC Regents announced Napolitano's appointment as president of the system, student protests erupted across the state (figure I.1). Undocumented students and allies were shocked and angry that the UC system would now be run by the person who—in her capacity as the head of DHS—had overseen thousands of deportations of migrants. By way of response, in her first major speech as president Napolitano pledged thousands of dollars for undocumented students and their families in the UC system in the form of financial aid, campus programming, and legal support.[2] Then, in the spring of 2015, she spearheaded the first National Summit on Undocumented Students, an event that would bring undocumented students from each of the nine UC campuses to Oakland, where they would hear from university administrators, politicians, and some of the most prominent legal advocates for migrant rights at the state and federal levels. Anahí was selected as one of the student representatives from UC Riverside to attend the summit.

A quick plane ride from Southern California delivered her to the San Francisco Bay Area in the late afternoon with some of the other students from Riverside who would be attending the event. Many, like her, were involved in PODER, but there were some that she was meeting for the first time. At the Oakland Marriott, where the summit was being held, Anahí's excitement grew. She was meeting dozens of other undocumented students from across the UC system. She had known some of them through their online presence, and now she was able to interact with them in person. Underneath this current of excitement, Anahí could also feel a communal sense of discomfort and even suspicion. Speaking with one another, they realized that the UC Office of the President (UCOP) had planned the sum-

I.1   UC Riverside newspaper coverage of students protesting the appointment of Janet Napolitano as president of the UC system.

mit largely without input from students. Students from some campuses had no idea how their representatives had been chosen; they worried that it was not a good representative cross-section of undocumented students' experiences. Others questioned the impressive lineup of speakers. Despite their high profiles as lawyers, scholars, and policy advocates, few could speak to the experience of being undocumented. It seemed to be a summit about undocumented students, but not *for* them.[3] Perhaps most acutely, many students felt deep discomfort that the summit was credited to Napolitano. Still feeling the sting of her appointment to the position of president of the UC system, some students felt wary, if not outright betrayed, that she was at the helm of the college education that they would receive. They believed that this summit was simply a public relations event for Napolitano to heal the perception that she was anti-immigrant, especially given the racially and ethnically diverse student demographics at the UC's nine campuses.

That evening, Anahí joined several of her peers to vent their frustration about the planning and intent of the summit. Twenty or thirty of them sat shoulder to shoulder in one of their hotel rooms at the Marriott. Articulating their frustration in community turned into a decision to mount a protest. The UC Office of the President had not asked them what they wanted out of the summit; this was a way for them to make their voices heard.

They decided that they would disrupt Napolitano's opening comments the next morning—the first morning of the official program. They would stand with their fists in the air when Napolitano began to speak. *Would they all be facing her?* No, they would turn their backs to her to respond symbolically to how she had turned her back on them in planning the summit. They would deliver a speech of their own. *How many people would speak?* One from each campus to demonstrate that this was truly a collective action. *What about the student representatives who had not yet arrived?* Students would tell peers from their own campuses about the protest before the program began and let them decide whether or not they would participate. *Who would write the speech?* The students nominated one person from each UC school to read out the speech. These people would stay behind to write it that evening.

Anahí's first impulse was to volunteer to be the student from UC Riverside who would speak. It was the end of her first year at the university, and she had already been very involved with PODER. She had helped plan events; she had publicly delivered her personal testimonio about how she came to be undocumented. But in that room, even alongside so many other undocumented students, she hesitated. Anahí understood that the protest was being planned because she and her fellow students wanted to feel a greater sense of inclusion in the summit. If they were to participate in it, the event had to be more than a public relations event for Napolitano. But she also knew that the action was a way for them to stand up to the woman who, as head of the DHS, had authorized thousands of deportations, including her father's. Anahí felt enough anger and indignation to want to be part of the action, but she also felt fear. They would be protesting the *president* of the UC system. She was not sure that she would be able to deliver her portion of the speech without faltering. She might cry. Anahí knew that even though she was outwardly engaged, she still carried with her the image of that white van taking her father away. She could easily tell people that she was undocumented. But she could not say that she was unafraid. Not yet.

Anahí decided not to volunteer to read out UC Riverside's part of the speech. Her friend Mafalda, who was a third-year student and an officer in PODER, would be a good representative for the university.[4] She knew that she could lean on this community to do what they needed to do together, and this allayed some of her fear. Anahí felt nervous excitement when she returned to her hotel room that night because she knew that, even though she wouldn't be speaking, she and her peers would make a statement the next day that would reverberate across the state.

Though I would not find out about the protest until the next morning, I arrived at the UC Undocumented Student Summit in Oakland the evening that Anahí and her peers were planning it. Years later, I would call Anahí to ask her perspective of the summit action. Instead, she told me about the day ICE raided her home. For her, a significant part of the protest was deciding not to be the Riverside speaker, a decision that was directly connected to the residual trauma from her father's deportation. This was important for me to understand because it was a reminder that there are always personal, unseen undercurrents to each large-scale political action. Student activism in California has had a significant impact on university policy toward its undocumented students. It demonstrates a powerful way that students can leverage their education and position as college students to enact change. Within this movement, however, are individual students whose activism is rooted in intimate connections to their families and communities.

This book explores the intersections between education and activism among undocumented students involved at UC Riverside. It examines how students' experiences in college—both in and outside the classroom—can affect their activism and advocacy work. Conversely, it also looks at how activism and advocacy work can be seen as an educational project. In my analysis, I take an expansive view of education. In addition to what students learn in their college classrooms, I include knowledge they gain from their families, communities, and peers, as well as from student and political organizations. In these different spaces, students learned how to navigate community and, later, college life as undocumented people; they were learning about immigration and education policy in practice—the social, economic, and political limits imposed on them because of their legal status. These lessons began at home and were deepened in college spaces. Student and political organizations were integral to undocumented education because they cultivated students' leadership skills and helped students understand that they were not alone. These organizations provided much needed community to undocumented young people and helped students to understand that their individual experiences of illegality (e.g., being unable to get a driver's license, the deportation of a parent) were part of a larger structure of legal violence. This type of education empowered students to make their way to and through college.

The undocumented students I worked with did not solely receive education. They grappled with it; they embodied it; and, most important, they mobilized it through social and political action. A key part of the work of members of PODER was to teach others what they had learned and to pay it forward. These were often practical educational projects, such as how to fill out a financial aid application or hosting Know Your Rights workshops. More profoundly, however, were their public-facing actions about specific political demands and the desire to be recognized as fully human. These actions included protests, such as the one at the UC Undocumented Student Summit, where students forced the UC president to recognize what they actually needed from the university system. They also included public events where students would share testimonios, personal stories that served as "counternarratives" to dispel narrow and negative stereotypes about the undocumented migrant community and where they could make known their humanity.

These educational interventions were particularly important within the context of an increasingly neoliberal university system. Within institutions where diversity among undergraduate students has become a kind of capital, undocumented students are viewed as adding value to the university because of the traumas and hardships they have endured while still managing to be "high-achieving" or "Dreamers."[5] Administrators often laud university diversity but are not always committed to addressing the needs of such students. This includes conceptualizing how university cultures should change to be more inclusive. Gabrielle Cabrera argues that when undocumented student activists push back against their tokenization by university they are "self-making their own subjectivity."[6] This was particularly apparent during the UCOP protest. In that moment, undocumented students insisted that Napolitano hear their concerns: their continued legal precarity, the false binaries between good and bad immigrants, the fallacy of undocumented students as "Dreamers" when their parents were criminalized. Students at the summit refused to be "good"; rather, they demanded to be seen in their full humanity. We can understand their action at the summit as a teaching moment, a lesson to university administrators.

Lessons about policy, how to live in the United States as an undocumented person, and the advocacy work that included demands for dignity all constitute what I came to understand as undocumented education. This education is undocumented because it is education for undocumented people. It is also undocumented because it is often informal and unsanctioned by the university. Undocumented education encompasses the ways that undocumented young people learn, both in formal settings and in their families and communities. Undocumented education often has deeply personal and high stakes. Knowledge about immigration and education policies and how to manage "illegality" can affect both quality of life and life paths for many undocumented people. Undocumented education is not stagnant; rather, it shifts to respond to the political moment or an individual's political consciousness. Like all education, undocumented education can be mobilized. It also posits that undocumented young people's advocacy work and activism is inherently pedagogical. Education is an integral part of political work and, ultimately, social transformation.

This work builds on and is deeply influenced by critical scholarship in education, anthropology, Chicanx studies, and ethnic studies that has shed light on the life circumstances of undocumented youth. In this book, I rely on theoretical frameworks that include multigenerational punishment, pedagogies of home, community cultural wealth, the politics of deserving-ness, and undocumented legal consciousness to interpret and analyze the situations of students in PODER. At its heart, however, this book is about the limits and the possibilities of education to humanize undocumented communities. I draw primarily from the Brazilian scholar Paulo Freire's ideas about education and its potential for social change. Specifically, Freire's *Pedagogy of the Oppressed* provided an important way for me to understand the knowledge that students gain from their families and communities before they set foot in any college classrooms. Freire's problem-posing model of education helped me more deeply comprehend how critical educational spaces could validate students' existing knowledge and build on it through an exchange of ideas. It also provided the basis for me to recognize how students could be teachers to others at the university and in other public spaces. Finally, and perhaps most important, Freire's model of educational praxis—reflection, theory, action—provided the blueprint for me to see how undocumented students mobilized their education in an effort to create a better world for themselves, their families, and their communities.

"You Can't Leave a DACA Clinic These Days without Three People Trying to Get You to Fill Out Their Survey": Methodological Considerations

Though I had known students who were active in PODER and had attended their annual scholarship banquets, at the beginning of the fall of 2013 I did not know any of the group's current members. I scheduled a meeting with the group's new president to discuss the possibility of research with PODER. She had come to my office and was sitting in the same blue chair students used for office hours, directly across from me. When I finished telling her about my idea for research, she said, "You can't leave a DACA clinic these days without three people trying to get you to fill out their survey." She wanted to know what benefit students might see from my work. Her comment startled me, but it made me reflect on the timing of this project. Deferred Action for Childhood Arrivals (DACA), the Obama-era executive action that offered limited protection from deportation for certain undocumented youth, had been in effect for just over a year, and the program had gained the attention of researchers. Until that moment, it had not occurred to me that undocumented young people might be experiencing research fatigue; that they might be tired of being "studied." I would be doing fieldwork and interviews with students, not survey research, but I knew that she was asking me for something more.

Undocumented college students understand that research is important. It gives college administrators and politicians data to advocate for important policies such as DACA and inclusive financial aid. At a certain point, however, it is exhausting to give energy and time to researchers you are likely never to see again. It was not enough for me to say that my research would help people better understand the situation of undocumented students. I would have to consider what it would mean to act ethically as a researcher and how to be responsive to students' unique positionalities and needs.

In considering the ethical imperatives of working with undocumented students, I was influenced by discourses around decolonial anthropology, Indigenous research imperatives, and activist anthropology. While decolonial anthropology calls for researchers to disrupt power relations, I knew that I could not shed my privileges as a citizen—someone who has never experienced life without papers—and as a professor in a student space. Once the members of PODER welcomed me to the group's meetings and events, I positioned myself as an ally and as someone who was there to learn. I tried to make sure that the voices of undocumented members of the group, and then their student allies, were heard first. Listening was not solely about "observing" in the traditional anthropological model of participant observation. Responding to decolonial and Indigenous scholars, I listened to understand the issues that were most pressing for my students and then to adjust my research questions accordingly.[7] My primary interest was how undocumented college students leveraged their education in their activist work. During my time with students, however, I heard students speak consistently about their families. There was a clear desire to disrupt the deserving "Dreamer" narrative that had emerged over the previous decade that seemed to position them against their parents, who were often rendered as "undeserving."[8] Students' concerns about their undocumented parents pushed me to include their families in my research, analyzing how pedagogies of home were a key component of undocumented education.

In addition, I knew that I was not simply going to be an observer in the group. When I asked permission to research PODER members' activities, I told them that I could offer my perspective as a professor—my knowledge of university bureaucracy, as well as my institutional knowledge. When appropriate, then, I offered my opinions and advice. Given that this research was with a politically vulnerable community, I also made an effort to align my approach with activist anthropological research. Shannon Speed defines activist anthropology as "the overt commitment to an engagement with our research subjects that is directed toward a shared political goal."[9] In this case, the goal is increased rights and resources for undocumented students on campus, as well as the broader struggle for migrant rights in the US public sphere. This meant that in administrative spaces I was an advocate for students. When the federal government announced the termination of the DACA program in September 2017, I was at demonstrations along with current and former students. I would be learning from those events, but I was also present to add my voice to the protests.

More than activist anthropology, however, my methodology is better described as research acompañamiento. The concept of acompañamiento has been used in theology, as well as in education and anthropology contexts. I rely most directly on work by the education scholar Enrique Sepúlveda, who outlines the ways that acompañamiento can be used both as a pedagogy and as a research approach when working with migrant and undocumented youth. Drawing from the liberation theologian Roberto Goizueta, Sepúlveda describes acompañamiento as a praxis that includes being with another, as well as feeling and doing with another.[10] My research with undocumented students was inherently relational. In attending their meetings and events, I came to know them not just as members of a group, but as individuals with particular life situations and trajectories. I shared in their moments of struggle and joy, and they shared in mine. Acknowledging my privilege as a citizen who was a professor at a university where they were students, I was intentional about being in community with the students in PODER. As Sepúlveda writes, "In the process of liberation, the voices of those on the margins must be recentered. Strong communities are sustained by authentic and supportive relationships that cut across all spheres, often including allies from more privileged backgrounds."[11] I wanted students to be able to use my allyship as a way to further their political and educational goals. I also understood that community building was a central part of the radical humanizing possibilities of undocumented education.[12]

When I proposed to work with PODER in the fall of 2013, I delivered a presentation explaining my research to the group at one of its regular meetings. After members asked me some questions about my methodology and how I would use the information that I gathered, I left the meeting so that they could deliberate whether and how they would participate. The president contacted me the next day to tell me that the group had decided to give me full access to their meeting spaces and permission to attend their events. Individual students would decide whether or not they wanted to consent to interviews. With this consent, between 2013 and 2015, I attended the group's weekly meetings, student conferences, public actions, talking circles, presentations at local high schools, socials, and annual scholarship banquet. During that time, I interviewed eighteen students—most currently enrolled, but also some alumni—to better understand the group's history and trajectory. These interviews were semi-structured and focused on individual life stories and perspectives about education and activism in broad terms. Similar to the decolonial interviewing process that Carolina Alonso Bejarano, Lucia López Juárez, Mirian Mijangos García, and Daniel Goldstein deployed in *Decolonizing Ethnography*, when issues or problems arose in the interview about the need for educational or legal support, I would try to direct students to university and community resources.[13] Chicano/a and Undocumented Student Affairs staff invited me, as an ally, to take part in meetings between students and the Office of the Vice Chancellor of Student Affairs when they were creating a budget for institutionalized undocumented student support. In those meetings, I witnessed undocumented student advocacy and learned more about what they needed from the university.

By the 2015–16 school year, I felt as if I had a strong sense of the rhythm of PODER: the group's major events throughout the year and the smaller events in which it participated. At that time, I decided to wind down my fieldwork, conducting just a few interviews and attending fewer events. Even as my research was ending, I continued to meet students for meals and coffee, sometimes hosting them in office hours. Many were graduating and wanted to talk about their next steps; I was invested in continuing to accompany them as they transitioned to the subsequent stages of their lives. I was compelled to pick up my research again after the 2016 presidential election, knowing that I needed to understand how that dramatic political event affected the students and their approach to advocacy. I began to attend meetings and events again, though not as consistently. I attended several protests, attended meetings, and sometimes spoke publicly to advocate for sanctuary for immigrants on campus and in the city of Riverside. This type of advocacy work in research is consistent with the activist anthropology detailed by Charles Hale and Shannon Speed, but I was primarily there because of my own political beliefs and to stand alongside—acompañar—the students I had come to know and care about.[14] A new generation of PODER students was emerging, but my primary relationships were with the cohort that graduated in the mid-2010s. I ended my fieldwork in 2017, except for the occasional follow-up interview. My relationships with former members of PODER continue to this day.

The ethnography in this book is primarily based on interviews and field research. To write about the events that students recounted to me but I did not personally witness, I drew from additional primary and secondary sources. The storytelling in these chapters might read like Clifford Geertz's "thick description."[15] However, I consider the writing more akin to that of feminist anthropologists who blur the lines of ethnography and creative nonfiction to critique objectivism and capture the emotional force of people's stories.[16] This style of ethnographic writing also heeds calls of Chicanx studies scholars to write in a way that is accessible to community members outside of the academy. As an extension of my methodological approach into my writing, all of the students I write about in this book have had the opportunity to read and comment on drafts of the ethnography that pertains to them. This was done for accuracy and to ensure that my research continued to be accountable to the students who shared their stories with me.

Structure of the Book

This book is divided into two sections. The first (chapters 1–2) explores the idea of undocumented pedagogies of home, lessons young people learn from their families about immigration policy and policing, as well as about work ethic and advocacy. The second section (chapters 3–5) looks at the kinds of education undocumented students receive in college—both in and outside the classroom—and how this education informs and shapes their advocacy and activism. Taken together, the chapters reveal the many sites of education for undocumented young people and the ways young people can mobilize political knowledge.

Chapter 1 is about the undocumented migration of a parent. It is rare that the discourses around undocumented migration and undocumented student education intersect, but young people are often deeply affected by their parents' migration stories. While most of the students I interviewed did not remember their own migration, they knew their parents' migration stories well. Stories of undocumented migration in a family were primary lessons about border policy and policing. The story that I highlight in chapter 1 also shows the intimate connections between a father facing a harrowing unauthorized border crossing while his son, a college student, awaited news for him on the other side. This migration story provided an all-too-intimate understanding of border militarization.

Chapter 2 uses pedagogies of home as a theoretical framework to understand how undocumented parents educate their children, especially in light of under-resourced schools and anti-immigrant policies.[17] It examines implicit lessons, such as modeling good work ethics, as well as providing students with an understanding of labor exploitation among the undocumented working class, which helps to build aspirational capital. The chapter also details the explicit lessons that parents teach their children about policing, racial profiling, and advocacy, which help to build their navigational capital. Even though some of these lessons are shaped by structural violence, I argue that students grapple with the education that they receive at home and that, ultimately, these pedagogies of home set the stage for the development of students' political identities in college.

The second section opens with a chapter about how two undocumented students develop political consciousness in college and become advocates for the undocumented community. It highlights the role that Latinx student organizations play in creating safe space for undocumented students and how peers can teach one another about social issues and imagine a different social reality. These student-oriented spaces were critical to the undocumented political education of the two young people highlighted in chapter 3. Chapter 4 more deeply explores how undocumented young people mobilize their political knowledge. In that chapter I demonstrate how, through their advocacy and activism, students teach others about the experiences of being undocumented in this country and the stakes of immigration policy and push to change common understandings and ideologies about the undocumented migrant community, as well as for pro-migrant policies.

Chapter 5, the final chapter, examines the aftermath of the 2016 presidential election within the undocumented student community at UC Riverside. The election results sent waves of fear and anxiety through the undocumented student community as they and their families began to make contingency plans in the event of mass deportations. It forced students to mobilize their education to advocate for their communities in a more defensive way. That moment also brought to bear the importance of community and the primary goal of human dignity. The epilogue of the book presents an ethnographic vignette of Raza Graduation in which one undocumented student reflects on her educational journey and her hopes for the future.

The Summit

It was just after eight o'clock in the morning when I approached the open doors of the Oakland Marriott ballroom. As I stepped inside, I saw a vast room full of people dressed in blazers, pencil skirts, and collared shirts. They were seated around white-tableclothed tables, on maroon-padded chairs, with well-heeled shoes resting on the giant swirls of the autumn colored carpet. Most noticeable, however, were the dozens of students with their fists in the air and backs turned toward Janet Napolitano, who was standing at podium in the front of the room. She was silent even though she had the microphone, and it was the students who were speaking. Nine students—one from each campus—were standing on ballroom chairs, facing Napolitano and projecting their voices so that she and everyone else in the room could hear.

"We are not here to simply fill these seats for your political gain!"

Though the early May day outside was cold and gray, the university administrators, staff, policy makers and advocates, and, especially, student protesters in the room were bathed in the golden light streaming from the elegant light fixtures above. The students had disrupted the UC president's

I.2   Students protest the UC National Summit on Undocumented Students in May 2015. Courtesy of Mafalda Gueta.

opening remarks (figure I.2), and though there was tension in the room, there was also a current of energy. The students were forcibly reorienting the summit to their needs and concerns.[18]

I recognized Mafalda, one of the students from UC Riverside, as he read out his part of the speech: "In your own words Ms. Napolitano, 'may these next two days result in positive, action-oriented DISCUSSIONS' and not just polished and practiced soundbites that skew the reality of the struggles we face."

The final student speaker ended the speech by saying, "We demand that you LISTEN to us," then shouted, "Undocumented!"

"Unafraid!" the student collective shouted in response. I then watched in awe as the students—the speakers and those who had their backs turned—began to stream out of the room. I saw Anahí and Mafalda, students I knew from PODER, as well as others whom I would meet and get to know better over the next two days and several months. There were no smiles; there was no chatter—just quiet determination as they walked into the outside light.

1

THE ORIGINAL DREAMERS

In the wake of a family tragedy, Jorge's parents and siblings left Orange County, California—one by one over a year and a half—to return to their hometown in central Mexico. Jorge stayed behind to continue his studies at the University of California (UC), Riverside, certain that he'd be able to complete the final five quarters he needed to earn his bachelor's degree. After nine months without his family's financial and emotional support, however, Jorge found himself struggling. This was painfully apparent to Jorge's father, Sergio, every time they spoke on the phone or exchanged text messages. Increasingly concerned about his son's well-being, Sergio decided to return to the United States; his son needed him. Without the financial or social characteristics that would qualify him for a visa, Sergio would have to migrate without legal authorization.

Sergio told Jorge that he would be traveling through a part of the Arizona desert where few people crossed, but not to worry. He would leave at night with a small group, and the journey would take only a few hours under the cover of darkness. Jorge had heard about the dangers of crossing through the desert: that people got lost in the rough terrain; that the sun was punishing; and that migrants often died of dehydration. Despite Sergio's attempts to ease his mind about the journey, Jorge was anxious about his father's safety. That night passed and then another, and Jorge still had no news of his father. He continued to attend classes and go through the motions of his regular life as a college student, but he was deeply worried. When a week had passed, Jorge received a phone call from an Orange County phone number. A voice at the other end of the line said, "We have your dad. He's with us in Santa Ana. Come pick him up and bring money." Unsure whether the threat was legitimate, Jorge called a family friend in Orange County, who told him she doubted that his father had arrived yet. A couple of days later, Jorge received another call. "Give us the money, or we're going to kill your dad." Relatively confident that he was being scammed, Jorge replied, "I think that you have the wrong number."

Jorge decided to call his mother in Mexico to see whether she had heard anything from his dad. His mother was as worried as he was, but she was also angry.

"Whatever happens to your dad is your fault," she told him bitterly. Jorge could hear his older sister in the background echoing the sentiment. "Tell him it's his fault." They didn't understand why Jorge had insisted on staying in California when the rest of his family returned to Mexico. If it weren't for Jorge's stubbornness, Sergio would not be missing.

Without saying anything, Jorge ended the call. For days afterward, the shock and sting of his mother's words affected him. He tried to cry, but he could not. He alternated between feeling guilt that something might have happened to his father and anger at his mother. She and his sister had seen him struggle to learn English; they witnessed his deep disappointment when he realized the family had no way to pay for him to attend a four-year university after high school. He thought they would understand how important it was for him to finish his college degree.

A few days later Jorge received a third phone call.

"Is this Jorge?" a male voice asked him in Spanish.

"Yeah."

"I'm calling because your dad gave me your number. We left him behind. He couldn't walk anymore."

"What do you mean?"

"We left him behind about two hours ago."

Jorge asked the man on the phone their exact location, but he didn't know where they were or where they had left his father.

Two days passed. By this time, it was finals week, and all of Jorge's peers were consumed with a different kind of worry. In this final push toward the end of the quarter, the libraries were full. All his peers seemed to be coming from or heading to study sessions.

He received another phone call. A man's voice said, "I'm in a little town on the edge of the desert. Do you think that you can find somebody to pick me up?"

Jorge wondered whether this was another kind of scam. He strained to hear traces of his father's voice in this man's tired speech, but he couldn't. He told the man that he had the wrong number.

The man insisted, "I am your dad, and I need somebody to come and pick me up. Can you have somebody come and pick me up?"

Jorge considered that the man wasn't asking for money; he was asking to be rescued. He decided that he would take a chance.

Intimate Connections

"Tell me your migration story." I began each interview I conducted for this project with that open-ended question. Because many of the students I interviewed were too young to remember the conditions of their crossing, they often told me stories that were recounted to them by family members. Some didn't tell me their stories at all; rather, like Jorge, they told the stories of their parents' crossing. Telling their family members' migration stories as their own is significant because it illustrates how the experience of migration becomes part of a family's collective consciousness.[1] Though the young people in my study often did not have personal recollections of the conditions of their crossing, their parents' stories—often told repeatedly over the years—became a kind of collective experience that led them to a particular understanding of the world. Family stories shape how undocumented young people see the world and their place in it. These migration narratives often illustrate the brutal conditions of crossing an increasingly militarized border, and they demonstrate the close relationships between the person who is crossing and members of their family who wait for news of a safe arrival. When Jorge recounted his father's story of crossing the border, I understood the treacherous conditions of the Arizona desert. What also came into sharp relief for me was the fact that even though Jorge did not cross the border under these conditions, he felt the mental and emotional impact of crossing. The weight and trauma of border militarization reached him, even as a college student entering into a period of final exams.

Drawing from Jorge's story, this chapter illustrates the intimate connections between adult migrants and their young adult children, often referred to as "Dreamers." It demonstrates how their lives are often inextricably intertwined and that anti-immigrant policies meant to target adult migrants also indelibly affect undocumented young people. Finally, this chapter shows a key aspect of undocumented education: migrant families learn about immigration policy through lived experience. The public might learn about laws that are debated in Congress in the abstract through various forms of media. For undocumented people, however, these laws are not abstract. Rather, they powerfully shape their lives and the lives of their children.

I draw from Genevieve Negrón-Gonzales, Leisy Ábrego, and Kathleen Coll's discussion of immigrant "deservingness" to elucidate public perceptions of undocumented migrant adults and undocumented youth.[2] They write, "Deservingness sets the rubric against which society determines the worthiness of immigrants to access basic human rights."[3] These scholars focus their work on the problematic distinctions made between undocumented young people who are rendered more worthy of citizenship or protection from deportation than other youth. Immigrants' worthiness can be understood in a variety of ways, but the easiest way to understand the good immigrant characteristics is to look at the eligibility requirements for Deferred Action for Childhood Arrivals (DACA). To qualify for DACA, undocumented youth must be enrolled in school, have graduated from high school, received a general education diploma (GED), or served honorably in a branch of the US military. Furthermore, they must demonstrate that they are of good "moral character," not having been convicted of a felony or serious misdemeanor or any misdemeanor more than three times. In short, strong academic performance or willingness to serve in the armed forces renders migrants deserving of the legal protections offered by DACA. Negrón-Gonzales and her colleagues introduce the framework of deservingness to theorize and highlight the false divisions between so-called deserving immigrant youth and those undocumented young people who are not seen as deserving in the public imagination.

In this chapter, I extend their framework to illustrate how the state extends leniency to undocumented college students (based on so-called deservingness) while enacting punitive measures toward their undocumented parents. Adult migrants are often criminalized for their choice to cross the border without papers; their children are absolved of this crime because they did not choose to migrate. Implicit in the discourse around deservingness are considerations of class. The logic is that upwardly mobile immigrant youth deserve legal protections, but their working-class parents do not. The ideology of immigrant deservingness elides the long history of Mexican migration to the United States, which largely has been based on the US desire for exploitable labor. Despite the country's dependence on migrant labor, the state rarely offers legal protections to migrant workers. Throughout the twentieth century, and now in the twenty-first century, we have seen what Nicholas De Genova refers to as an "intricate history of law-making" that renders some migrants "illegal" while granting protections to others.[4] Historians such as Mae Ngai and Cristina Salinas have illustrated that throughout the twentieth century US laws have rendered Mexican migrants legally vulnerable, if not outright "illegal."[5] US Border Patrol agents have looked the other way when farmers have needed Mexican labor to pick crops in Texas and California while simultaneously drawing attention to a "spectacle" of migrants at border points of entry. This continues to occur through today as our immigration laws do not match our economic needs. Meanwhile Mexican adult migrants are racialized as social, economic, and legal threats to the nation.[6]

By contrast, the Dreamer discourse that emerged around the year 2000 placed young undocumented migrants in a different position—one of deservingness. The word *Dreamer* refers to undocumented young people who would have benefited from the federal Development, Relief, and Education for Alien Minors (DREAM) Act; they were often represented as a "blameless," Americanized generation of migrant youth graduating from high school with limited access to higher education and few job opportunities.[7] Their political profile and narratives appealed to conservatives and liberals alike, and their acts of civil disobedience were part of a carefully planned political strategy to pass the DREAM Act, one piece of what many immigrant rights advocates hoped would lead to comprehensive immigration reform.[8] While focusing on Dreamers made political sense, it unwittingly positioned them against those who had chosen to migrate for work.[9] If young people identified as Dreamers were blameless because they had not chosen to migrate without legal authorization, then their adult parents who made those decisions could be construed as guilty and not deserving of citizenship.

One of the first young people I interviewed for this project very clearly articulated her discomfort with the Dreamer narrative when she told me,

"Generally speaking, I did not like being involved in undocumented groups [at that time] just because they were a little . . . let's throw our parents under the bus sometimes."[10] Though that conversation happened in 2013, it continues to resonate with me. Even now that the migrant justice movement has largely moved away from the strategy of presenting undocumented young people as Dreamers, most Americans do not understand the intimate connections between undocumented adults and their children—children who are both undocumented and American-born. It is often the same criminalized "aliens" who are raising Dreamers.[11]

The relationship between these two generations of undocumented migrants is at the heart of this chapter, which aims to show not only the intimate connections between the two, but also the way that restrictive immigration policies affect both cross-sections of the community. I draw from Laura Enriquez's concept of multigenerational punishment to understand this phenomenon. Enriquez defines multigenerational punishment as the process by which "sanctions intended for a specific population spill over to harm individuals who are not targeted by immigration policies."[12] She primarily uses multigenerational punishment to understand how immigration policy affects citizen children of undocumented adults. I extend her analysis to examine how immigration policy affects the 1.5 generation who crossed the border as children. Specifically, the border-militarization policies and practices deployed in the 1990s were not necessarily intended to affect undocumented college students. Jorge's story illustrates that border militarization fails to keep migrants from crossing; instead, it creates treacherous conditions for migrants and affects subsequent generations of their families. When Jorge's father crossed the border in December 2009, Congress was considering a federal DREAM Act that would have provided a pathway to citizenship for undocumented young people like Jorge. However, the promise of a DREAM Act was not the immigration policy that most affected Jorge's life. His life was being affected by 1990s-era border-militarization policies that created a situation in which the only way his father could return was by risking his life to cross the Arizona desert.

As a science major at UC Riverside, Jorge was not learning about US Immigration and Naturalization Service (INS) policies and practices along the US-Mexico border in his classes. However, as part of an undocumented family, Jorge and his father learned about these policies through their lived experiences. Migration stories form the basis of how undocumented young people and their families learn about border policy. Unlike the general public, they learn not only about the policies but also about how people experience policy. They learn about smugglers' increased fees; they learn about dangerous crossing routes; they learn about migrant death. Undocumented education, in this case, is how migrants learn about immigration policy through their bodily experiences—physically and psychologically. Though informal, learning in this way enables a deep understanding of how immigration policy affects families and communities.

Militarizing the Border

Prior to the passage of the Hart-Celler Act of 1965, no numerical restrictions were placed on people who wanted to migrate from the Western Hemisphere to the United States. Though largely seen as progressive legislation because it eliminated national origin quotas, the act limited the number of visas issued to Mexico for the first time ever. The historian Ana Raquel Minian argues that after the passage of the Hart-Celler Act, Mexicans who had witnessed generations of family members migrating back and forth to the United States to work now had limited to no legal pathway to cross the border themselves. Despite this new specter of illegality, because of Mexico's "surplus" labor force and US desire for cheap labor, Mexicans continued to migrate north over the next two decades.[13] When the Immigration Reform and Control Act (IRCA) was signed into law in 1986, thousands of Mexicans who were living without papers in the United States were able to legalize their status. This resulted in the permanent settlement of Mexicans north of the border and a temporary dip in the apprehension of undocumented people crossing.[14] Without a change in how visas were allocated, however, undocumented migration began to rise again in the early 1990s, leading to the public perception of an out-of-control southern border.[15] This set the stage for a different tactic to stymie undocumented migration from the south.

Beginning in 1993, the US Border Patrol began to fortify the US-Mexico border at traditional points of entry for undocumented migrants: the urban areas of El Paso, Texas, and San Diego, California, as well as the rural regions of southern Arizona and the Rio Grande Valley of Texas. The first initiative, Operation Hold the Line, was the brainchild of Silvestre Reyes, chief of the El Paso Sector of the Border Patrol. The initial strategy involved positioning hundreds of Border Patrol agents along the urban line of the El Paso border, as well as deploying low-flying helicopters to regularly traverse the skyline of the city, which was known as the Ellis Island for Mexican migrants at the turn of the twentieth century. This performance of policing was successful, at least in terms of pushing migrants to the outskirts of the city, where they were less visible to urban border dwellers. It also solved the problem of Border Patrol agents accidentally arresting brown-skinned residents of El Paso who might be physically indistinguishable from their undocumented counterparts.[16] Pushing migrants out of sight of the city was seen as enough of a success that similar operations were deployed in subsequent years in San Diego, through Operation Gatekeeper (1994); in Arizona, through Operation Safeguard (1994 and 1999); and in southern Texas, through Operation Rio Grande Valley (1994).

Placing "boots on the ground" and deploying low-flying aircraft along narrow corridors of the more populated areas along the Rio Grande were the first steps toward what we now refer to as border militarization. In subsequent years, the Border Patrol began to use military-grade materials and tactics to police the region.[17] Along the most common crossing points it erected ten-foot-high steel fencing made from Vietnam War surplus corrugated steel landing mats. Just a few decades earlier, the mats had been used as portable landing pads for helicopters to touch down in occupied and war-torn territories of Vietnam. Because the landing mats were often solid steel, they obscured visibility on both sides of the border, creating what some viewed as a blight on the landscape. More than that, however, the new wall created a division between border communities where residents crossed to shop, dine, visit family, and engage in social life. Now, during evenings, high-intensity stadium-type lighting posted along the wall illuminated the length of a football field along both sides of the border. The eerie fluorescent light cast deep shadows between hills and behind the dry desert vegetation. The Border Patrol also began to use Vietnam-era infrared night scopes, motion-detecting sensors buried in the ground, and remote video-surveillance systems.[18] While these technologies are now dated, they were at the time beyond what regular police forces could access, setting a precedent for military-grade technologies to be used to police the border. These military-type interventions began to signal to the nation-state that the border might be understood as, at best, a spectacle, and, at worst, a war zone.[19]

In addition to fortifying the physical space of the border, also during the mid-1990s, the Border Patrol began to use technology to track migrants and criminalize those who repeatedly crossed without authorization. The INS used a computerized system of biometric scanning to process migrants who were apprehended while crossing, which involved photographing people and recording their fingerprints and other information in a database to more easily detect undocumented migrants.[20] Indeed, in 1996 President

Bill Clinton signed the Illegal Immigration Reform and Immigrant Responsibility Act (IIRIRA) into law, which made reentry after deportation a federal felony defense punishable by a fine and up to two years in prison. The IIRIRA also introduced three- and ten-year bars for those migrants who had lived in the United States without papers and then wanted to reenter with legal authorization.[21]

The impact of these militarization tactics has been costly to potential border crossers, in terms of both currency and human life. The price of hiring a coyote to help migrants cross into the United States skyrocketed from $700 in 1996 to $1,500 in 2001.[22] This data, collected by the immigration scholar Wayne Cornelius prior to 2001, is now more than twenty years old. When I present those numbers to my students who know people who have crossed without authorization over the past few years, they all tell me that it costs more. Their estimates are around $4,000, but a *New York Times* article published in 2018 records at least one coyote fee at $6,000.[23] The reason the costs have increased so dramatically is that the journey is now more arduous and dangerous, requiring not only a more skilled guide but often a team of people working in tandem.[24] The militarization of traditional points of crossing has pushed migrants to more desolate, rural areas, including Arizona's vast Sonoran Desert. Funneling migrants through this striking yet treacherous terrain was the intentional decision of Border Patrol officials, who viewed it as a strategy to stymie undocumented migration. Doris Meissner, the commissioner of the INS during the Clinton administration in the 1990s, stated, "We did believe that geography would be an ally for us. It was our sense that the number of people crossing through the desert would go down to a trickle once people realized what [it was] like."[25] Meissner and her colleagues were engaging in a strategy that would later be referred to as "prevention through deterrence." However, the desert did not prove to be a deterrent. Instead, from the late 1990s until today, thousands of migrants have died attempting to cross the border through Arizona.[26]

The geographical features of the Arizona border region have created a unique combination of legal and extralegal military and police presence. Border Patrol agents police the region by land and sky, and there is also an air force and marine presence in the southwestern part of the state, where the Barry M. Goldwater Air Force bombing range occupies a large swath of land for soldiers to practice military drills. Tribal police of the Tohono O'odham Nation guard against drug smugglers to the east along with agents from the US Drug Enforcement Administration. Finally, there are the occasional citizen militias, who, with the belief that the federal government is not doing enough, police the border on their own.[27] This means that for migrants, death from the elements is not the only danger. As the immigration scholar Gilberto Rosas reminds us, "Este no se cuenta la violencia" (It is not just danger; it is also violence).[28] Corrupt people in the smuggling chains, drug runners, and members of citizen militias are not beholden to the same federal oversight as US Border Patrol, but even encounters with the latter can end in violence for migrants making their way to the United States.

Migrant Choices

Jorge is originally from Estado de Mexico, a state in Central Mexico surrounding the western, northern, and eastern edges of Mexico City. His hometown was nestled in a valley flanked by mountains, including the fabled volcanoes Iztaccíhuatl and Popocatépetl. For most of his childhood, Jorge and his two siblings were raised by their paternal grandparents, as well as by aunts and uncles, while their parents lived and worked in the United States. Because his father, Sergio, was largely absent, it was Jorge's uncle, his dad's younger brother, who taught Jorge how to play soccer, took him to his first sporting events, and talked to him about growing up. His parents, who were working in the United States without legal authorization, would send money to their family back home to support their children, and they would visit once or twice a year for several weeks before returning north. Migration scholars refer to this pattern as circular migration, a common practice before the US-Mexico border became militarized during the mid- and late 1990s. Jorge's parents always promised that they would only be in the United States for a little longer, but "a little longer" became a common and unfulfilled refrain for most of his childhood.[29] They had been migrating back and forth for ten years, and Jorge remembers, by the time he was eleven he was spending only about three months each year with his father, Sergio.

Jorge's parents hoped to earn and save enough money to return to Mexico and live a financially stable life with their children. Unfortunately, low wages, high costs of living, and the regular remittances they sent made saving difficult, and they found themselves living apart from their children longer than they had anticipated. Moreover, it was nearing the end of the 1990s, and their traditional points of crossing from Mexico to the United States were becoming more closely guarded, making it more dangerous and expensive to make the trips home. Fewer trips to Mexico coupled with the painful, unfulfilled promise of reuniting their family led Jorge's parents to a decision: they would bring their three children to live with them in the

United States, where they would stay indefinitely.[30] After a decade apart, reuniting their fractured family outweighed the fact that they would all be living without papers.

As a preteen, Jorge was vividly aware of the life that he would be leaving to join his parents in California. He did not know when he would next see his grandparents or the uncle who had been a steadfast presence in his life. He had friends, a school. He played sports. Jorge knew that migrating without papers meant that he and his immediate family would be in the United States for the long term, which filled him with anxiety and sadness.[31] However, his desire to have a relationship with his parents, especially his father, tempered his sense of loss. While Jorge knew what he would be leaving behind in Mexico, he was less aware of what his life would be like in the United States, especially what it would mean to be undocumented.

In 1999, the family began to build a life together in a city in California's Orange County. Though Sergio did not have papers, he had established a successful landscaping business. Arriving in the country well after the US Supreme Court decision in *Plyler v. Doe* (1982), which stipulated undocumented young people had the right to attend public elementary and high schools, Jorge and his siblings were able to enroll in their neighborhood schools. Jorge entered sixth grade and, like many immigrant children, he had to adjust to the social norms and culture of the US school system. This included struggling to learn English on a campus with no English Language Learner program.[32] He made his way through his grade level with the help of teachers and students who translated for him. Though the language was challenging, he discovered a love of science; biology and chemistry were two of his favorite classes. Jorge was a dedicated student, and he was receptive to the messages he received in school that with hard work he could achieve his goals. He adopted the ethos of the American dream even as an undocumented student, his sense of belonging dictated and strengthened by the fact that he was learning alongside his US-born peers.[33] Jorge began to imagine the possibilities of a US education; if he continued to apply himself in the sciences, he might eventually become a doctor.

In high school, Jorge joined the Advancement via Individual Determination (AVID) program, which helped him to build his study skills and learn about the college admissions process.[34] If he followed the path his AVID counselors laid out for him, he would graduate from college. On weekends, Jorge worked alongside his father cutting yards, and during that time together Sergio would encourage his son to pursue his education so he wouldn't have to spend the rest of his life working outside. As Jorge neared the end of high school and began preparing college applications, he realized something that brought his academic plans to a halt: while other graduating seniors could apply for financial assistance to pay for college, because he was undocumented, he was not eligible for any form of federal or state financial aid.[35] The California State Assembly passed a bill in 2001 that made undocumented high school students in the state eligible for in-state tuition, but the cost of these public colleges and universities was still prohibitive for many working-class families.[36] Jorge was bitterly disappointed when his father told him that, though they were paying tuition for his sister to attend California State University, Fullerton, the family would be unable to pay college tuition for him, as well.

Sergio started his own business because he encountered difficulty finding work without papers. While his business did well enough to keep the family afloat and even to pay tuition for one of his children, he knew the limits he faced in the landscaping industry. It was physically taxing work that paid low wages; this was precisely why he encouraged his children to pursue an education. Though it was difficult to tell Jorge that he would be unable to pay his tuition to a four-year university, he hoped that his son would understand that this was part of being undocumented. They did not have access to the same resources as citizens, but they could find ways to work around their obstacles. They could still live good lives. Because Jorge began his life in the United States in school and alongside US-born peers, he had not yet had to come to terms with his legal status in the same way that his father had.[37] All at once he felt the possibilities for his future constricting, imagining doors that were once open to him closing one by one.

Without divulging his situation to them, Jorge began to shut down the AVID counselors who encouraged him to apply for college; he no longer saw the point of working toward a goal that appeared out of reach. After several months, one of his counselors persuaded Jorge to register for courses at the local community college, actually taking him to the campus and helping him fill out the paperwork to enroll. Though he registered for the semester only half-heartedly, Jorge was quickly drawn into his community college classes. He was smart; he had always enjoyed learning; and his professors treated him and his peers as adults, which he appreciated. Jorge began to apply the same academic rigor to his classes as he had to his high school coursework. He steadily completed his breadth requirements, and during the middle of his second year at the community college, Jorge learned that he had fulfilled the requirements to transfer to a University of California school. By that time, his sister had stopped attending Fullerton, and Jorge's father told him that he could provide some financial support to transfer to a four-year university. When Jorge was admitted to UC Riverside as a neuroscience major in the spring of 2008, his plans for a career in medicine came back into focus.

As Jorge was completing his final courses at the community college that May, his maternal grandmother died. His mother was devastated that she wasn't in Mexico at the time of her mother's death and immediately began to make plans to return for the funeral. Though Jorge's father, Sergio, tried to persuade his wife to stay by telling her that they would be able to better help the family financially from the United States, to Jorge's mother it would be unconscionable to be away from her family at that moment. In reality, Sergio had also been thinking about returning to Mexico. That year the recession had taken a toll on his landscaping business. Once his wife left, Sergio waited for his two younger children to finish the school year and then sent them to be with her. Shortly after, Jorge's older sister decided to go to Estado de Mexico, as well. Within a month and a half, almost all of Jorge's family had returned to Central Mexico. Jorge and his father were the only ones who remained in California.

A New Beginning

At the end of the summer, Jorge left Orange County to begin school at UC Riverside. During the first few weeks of the quarter, still adjusting to campus, Jorge found himself in the middle of dozens of tables around the university bell tower. Students at each table were passing out flyers for their organizations, many talking and laughing among themselves. He walked through quickly, orienting himself toward the broad white arches in front of the library. He took his phone out of his back pocket to check a message when a young man from one of the tables called him over to let him know that he had dropped a $20 bill. He handed Jorge the bill, and they began to talk. He gave Jorge a flyer for a student organization—La Unión Estudiantil de la Raza (UER)—and invited him to the next meeting. Impressed by the gesture and curious about the group, Jorge decided to check it out.

He learned that UER had started in the mid-1990s to provide a space on campus where Latino students would feel welcome. It was oriented toward community service, focusing on issues that would help local Latino youth—such as providing backpacks at Thanksgiving and shoes at Christmas, hosting soccer clinics, and doing community repairs and clean-ups.

The group also promoted ethnic pride. Composed primarily of young men from Mexican and Central American families, UER focused on not only commonalities among their cultures, including language, but also histories of migration and generational struggle and sacrifice.[38] Jorge learned that the university considered the group a kind of Latino fraternity, but the members themselves resisted that label. They considered themselves a brotherhood, yes, but were more interested in creating a safe space, holding one another accountable to their work and studies, developing leadership skills, and, of course, doing community service. Jorge had not necessarily been looking for a group to join, but he could immediately sense that the brotherhood of UER would make his experience at UC Riverside better.

UER had connections to other student organizations on campus, especially those that drew support from the university's Office of Chicano Student Programs. One of these organizations was Providing Opportunities, Dreams, and Education in Riverside (PODER). During the fall quarter, PODER hosted its annual Dreaming of a Higher Education conference, and UER provided logistical support. Jorge joined his UER brothers in setting up signs that directed conference participants around campus; distributing box lunches; and providing help to presenters for their workshops throughout the day. As UER members prepared for the conference alongside the members of PODER, Jorge disclosed his status to some of the organizers. They immediately invited him to participate on a panel of current students who would speak to the experience of being undocumented at UC Riverside. He would be able to provide the perspective of a transfer student. Though Jorge was more of a listener than someone who was quick to speak, he agreed to participate. He liked the idea of being on a panel with other students who were making their way through college without papers, and he knew that he had something to contribute.

When, as a senior in high school, Jorge truly began to understand the ramifications of being undocumented, he was angry. He did not know that the foundation on which he had built his US life had been unstable because it was based on an incomplete and inaccurate understanding of his place in this country. At UC Riverside he was rebuilding, now with a clearer sense of what it meant to be undocumented in this country. Jorge had found a community at UC Riverside through his involvement with UER. Because of his previous experiences, he valued this new community and his place in it more than he might have otherwise. With the support of his new friends, Jorge could see his trajectory through college and toward a career.

Falling Apart

While Jorge was making friends and building community at UC Riverside, Sergio remained by himself in the house that the family rented in Orange County. The ongoing recession continued to hurt his landscaping business. Sergio was able to make ends meet and to help Jorge pay tuition, but he started to think that living in the United States might no longer make financial sense. By the end of November, the solitude coupled with his depressed business prospects weighed heavily on him. Sergio decided that he, too, would return to Estado de Mexico.³⁹ He reached out to Jorge, who was finishing his first quarter at UC Riverside, to talk to him about returning to Mexico. He tried to convince his son that it would be too difficult for a college student to live alone in the United States without the support of his family. When Jorge returned home for the Christmas holiday, their conversations turned into arguments. Jorge did not want to leave. He was happy at UC Riverside, and he didn't want to abandon his studies and his community. For Jorge, being at UC Riverside was the result of a decade's worth of effort to learn English, navigate the US education system, and then learn the latter all over again as an undocumented student. He was finally seeing the results of his studies, his efforts, and his struggles. Jorge wanted to make his father understand that if he were to return to Estado de Mexico, he would have to begin again.

His father tried to reassure him, saying, "We'll find a way over there." Jorge knew that his father had struggled with work in the United States but did not think his father understood US schools the way he did. They came to an agreement. Sergio would leave Jorge enough money to pay his college expenses for another quarter, with the understanding that Jorge would try to find a job. If all else failed, he could work on weekends and in the summer for some of Sergio's soon-to-be-former clients. They both knew that it would be a challenge, but Jorge was determined to stay. In January 2009, Sergio returned to Estado de Mexico, and Jorge returned to campus.

Winter quarter began as normal, with Jorge attending classes and participating in UER meetings and events. However, the money that his father left quickly ran out. Jorge was still ineligible for financial aid, and his legal status made it difficult for him to find flexible employment that would accommodate his school schedule. Three months after Jorge was advising high school students about how to navigate the UC system as an undocumented person, he found himself registering for the next quarter without knowing how he would pay for it. Fortunately for Jorge, a glitch in the computer system enrolled him in classes without placing a charge on his account. He continued to attend classes and his involvement with UER, but by the end of the school year his financial situation became more dire. He was no longer able to pay his rent. Three brothers from UER invited him to stay in their apartment. They didn't have a room for him, but they offered him their couch. On the verge of homelessness, Jorge gratefully accepted.

He tentatively registered for fall classes and was again enrolled without being charged. On weekends, Jorge had started to return to Orange County to do gardening work for some of his father's former clients using borrowed equipment. He would use that money to pay utilities at the apartment and rent textbooks. Then, a few weeks into the term, tragedy struck his family again: Jorge's uncle—the one who had been a surrogate father to him during the years of his childhood when his family lived apart—was killed outside a party in Estado de Mexico. The stress of family separation, dwindling finances, and the death of his uncle was too much. Jorge began to drink heavily to relax and unwind, but his grades started to slip. His friends continued to house him and even share groceries with him, but he had lost his equilibrium. He communicated with his family in Mexico through phone conversations and messages, but there was only so much support they could provide him from afar. Deeply worried about his son, Sergio decided to return to the United States. He would have to cross through the Sonoran Desert.

In the public eye, Jorge might be considered a Dreamer. He graduated from high school five years after the DREAM Act was introduced in Congress. This federal policy proposal would have granted temporary residency and a pathway to citizenship for undocumented young people who were brought to this country as minors.[40] Throughout the first decade of the twenty-first century, the federal DREAM Act failed time and again. In fact, Jorge matriculated at UC Riverside just one year after the US Senate failed to pass an incarnation of DREAM legislation, even with a simple majority.[41] Though it would have helped him, the proposed DREAM Act was not the policy that immediately affected Jorge; his life was more acutely affected by the ongoing deployment of the border-militarization policies of the 1990s. These inhumane and ineffective policies separated him from his family by making it treacherous for any of his family members to return to the United States from Mexico.

Family separation was the ongoing impact of border militarization that Jorge experienced during the year that his father returned to Mexico. That winter, however, a different aspect of these immigration policies weighed on him, inciting fear and anxiety while he was trying to complete his coursework for the term: the possibility that his father would die while crossing the desert trying to reach him. While the makers of immigration policy did not likely have young people such as Jorge—college students—in mind when they launched border-militarization initiatives, the ripple effects of these initiatives amounted to multigenerational punishment, affecting not only Sergio but also his son.

Crossing

It was the end of the fall quarter, just a few weeks before final exams, when Jorge learned that his father was going to attempt the return. He told only his closest friends—the three UER brothers who were sharing their apartment with him—that his father would be crossing the border. Otherwise, he kept everything to himself: the threatening phone calls, the conversation with his mother, and his feelings of anxiety and worry. To everyone else on campus—his professors, his classmates—he was just another student gearing up for the end of the quarter.

Jorge received the phone call from the person he thought might be his father while he was having dinner with one of his roommates. He got up from the table when the phone rang. In the moments after he ended the phone call, Jorge realized that he was going to need help. His father needed someone to pick him up in Arizona. Even if Jorge could borrow a car, he knew that the drive to Arizona would be too dangerous for him because he, too, was undocumented. In addition to US Border Patrol in southern Arizona, he had heard about the overzealous sheriffs in Maricopa County led by Joe Arpaio. Officers from either agency could easily detain him. If he were apprehended, he wouldn't be able to help his father. Jorge needed to find someone to drive to Arizona to pick up Sergio.

He knew the timing couldn't be worse. It was finals week, and everyone on campus was holed up in their rooms and in the libraries studying and preparing final papers and projects. Jorge also had finals, but they were the furthest thing from his mind; his immediate priority had to be finding a way to get his father to safety.

With all of these thoughts racing through his mind, Jorge sat back down to dinner with his friend.

"What's up?" the friend asked him.

The words came tumbling out. "My dad. He called me that he's here. He's in some town in Arizona, and he needs me to find someone to get him.

I can't go because of my situation. I need to get help. Is there anyone you think might be able to help me?"

His friend looked at him for a moment and said, "Well, I got finals tomorrow, but I'll go."

"Tomorrow after finals?"

"No, I'll go right now. Just let me get some stuff together."

Surprised and relieved, Jorge thanked his friend and watched as he prepared for the five-hour drive to Arizona. Within that short time, Jorge received another phone call from his dad.

"Hijo," he said. "Jesús is here in Arizona. Can you call him and ask if he can come pick me up? I don't have his number."

At that moment, Jorge was certain that it was his father on the other end of the line. No one else would know about this old friend of his dad's from Buena Park who had recently moved to Arizona. Though he was relieved to know that he was actually talking to his father, Jorge was not certain that Jesús would come through for them. Jesús and his father were friends, but they rarely saw eye to eye on political issues. Also an immigrant from Mexico, Jesús was more conservative than Jorge and his father on immigration issues. Jorge recalled hearing Jesús make comments that seemed—to him—borderline racist about migrants. He didn't think that Jesús would want to pick up his father, who had just crossed the border without legal authorization. Nevertheless, their options were limited. He made the call.

Jesús listened to Jorge explain the situation. Then he abruptly said, "I'll call you back right now. Let's not talk about this over the phone."

About fifteen minutes passed, and Jorge received a phone call from an Arizona area code. It was Jesús. "Give me the address, and I'll go get him."

Jorge spent the next three hours in the apartment waiting and wondering whether Jesús was really going to make the trip to pick up his father. Then he received a phone call from Sergio. He was safe at Jesús's house.

The Desert

Jorge expected that his father would be back in California that weekend; he didn't know how badly the trip through the desert had affected Sergio's physical health. The blisters on his feet alone prevented him from walking for almost a month. But in that time, through phone calls, Sergio was able to recount to his son how he crossed the desert.

Sergio had been abandoned by his group in the Arizona desert because he had become too weak to continue to walk with them. Disoriented, he dragged himself through spindly desert shrubs, kicking rocks and dust as he slowly moved along. Even in the winter, the white sunlight blanched the cacti and limbs of fallen trees. There was a hill pocked with small rocks in his line of vision, and he thought there might be something on the other side—a house, a town. *If I don't find anything, I'm just going to try to drag my body to where somebody can find it,* he thought. He heard a voice calling to him and saw another man in the distance. Sergio was convinced that he was hallucinating until the man reached him. The man was sunburned, and his clothing was thick with dust. Sergio learned that he was a drug smuggler who had been separated from his companion when the latter went in search of water. Though he did not seem to be in any condition to offer help, the smuggler told Sergio he would guide him to the nearest city for a price. Sergio agreed, and they set out together across the sun-bleached desert.

The two men finally came across an isolated ranch house. They walked across the arid front lawn and knocked. An older white woman cautiously opened the door and regarded them. They asked for water, but she closed the door quickly. Sergio didn't blame her; he hadn't seen a reflection of himself in days, but if he looked anything like his companion, he imagined that the woman would be nervous about their presence. He stood alongside his new friend, the smuggler, on the porch for a few minutes and discussed what their next steps should be. Then the door opened again. This time the woman was with her husband, and they offered the men bottles of water and chairs on the porch where they could rest. Because of his years in the United States, Sergio spoke English fairly well and was able to communicate with them. The woman and her husband told them that the area they had just crossed was an Air Force bombing range and that a group of migrants had recently been killed during a training exercise.[42] Even though the two men had survived the crossing, neither looked well. Sergio and the smuggler agreed to let the couple call for medical help.

Two paramedics arrived at the house within the hour, but they were hesitant to give medical attention to Sergio and his friend. They were in Maricopa County, where the elected sheriff, Joe Arpaio, was notorious for jailing migrants and instilling fear in those who would help them. They attended to Sergio and the smuggler at the house, and after some persuasion the paramedics agreed to transport them to the nearest town, Gila Bend.

The paramedics dropped the two men off in town, and Sergio and his friend began to look for a pay phone so they could call their mutual contacts for help. Their optimism about being rescued waned quickly when they spotted a sheriff's vehicle. Despite their efforts to look inconspicuous, the two men knew that their dust-caked clothes and badly sunburned faces betrayed them. The deputy drove up beside them and asked whether they were migrants.

"No," they told him. They were just returning from a day of work.

"Get in," he said, motioning to the police car.

Reluctantly, Sergio and his friend climbed into the backseat of his vehicle and, in spite of themselves, felt the comfort of the seats and the air conditioning. The sheriff's deputy handed them a couple of bottles of water and drove a few blocks to a nearby diner. They went inside, and the sheriff left them in a booth while he went to speak to one of the waitresses. The two men watched him leave the diner without looking back at them. They were pondering the sheriff's return when the waitress approached them to take their order.

"We don't have any money," Sergio told her.

"The sheriff already paid for your meals. He just doesn't want you to tell anyone that he helped you."

Grateful and relieved, the two men sank into the booth and ordered dinner.

Sergio had walked more than a hundred miles through the desert, and in another hour he would finally be able to call his son.

Another Beginning

It was about a month before Sergio was strong enough to travel again. Jesús, who still had a sister living in Orange County, offered to drive him to California. Nervous about the Immigration and Customs Enforcement (ICE) agents patrolling Interstate 10 and the checkpoint between Arizona and California, Jesús opted to drive a northwestern route that would take them through Laughlin, Nevada, before heading back south into California. Though this path added about 150 miles to their trip, Jesús felt it was the safest way to go. The inconvenience was a small price to pay. Sergio could feel the desert sun warming his arm through the passenger window and watched the blur of desert brush and rocky hillsides as they drove home. Even though he was protected from the elements in Jesús's air-conditioned car, Sergio knew that he would never regard the desert the same way again.

Meanwhile, Jorge was waiting for the phone call letting him know that his father had arrived in Orange County. When it finally came, Jorge left his Riverside apartment and made the forty-mile drive to Jesús's sister's house. He patiently drove through the pockets of traffic and imagined what he would say to his dad as he drove by the rolling hills that marked the southern end of Riverside County. As he entered the familiar landscape of Orange County, with its tangle of freeways and shopping centers speeding past, he navigated easily to Jesús's sister's house. She opened the door and ushered him through the house to the backyard. The yard was expansive, with mature fruit trees already heavy with citrus in the mild California winter. Jorge saw his dad and Jesús sitting and talking at a small table in the shade.

When he saw his father, Jorge felt his throat tighten. In his memory his father was always a strong man. Sergio was a landscaper. Even when he had been working under the sun for hours a day, his body was easily able to push a mower across a lawn, stretch and bend to tame unwieldy hedges or pull stubborn weeds. But this version of his father—a month since his travail through the desert—was small and frail-looking.

Jorge couldn't help but think how much worse his father's condition must have been a month earlier. His mother's words still echoed in his mind: *Whatever happens to your dad is your fault.* Guilt expanded in his chest. His father had returned for him. This man he barely knew until age eleven had risked his life to make sure that Jorge could be safe and have the life that he wanted. Jorge didn't know what to say. Sergio stood, and Jorge wrapped his arms around him, feeling his father's thin body against his own. He let out his breath as a long exhale, feeling more relaxed than he could remember feeling in a long time. He was with his dad again.

After a moment, Sergio pulled back, looked at Jorge, and asked, "How've you been? Are you OK?"

Jorge almost laughed. With Jesús and his sister watching their reunion, Jorge gave his father another long hug.

Though Sergio had returned to the United States to support his son as he completed his college education, Jorge was no longer able to register for classes at UC Riverside. The computer glitch that had enabled him to continue to enroll in courses had finally been corrected, and the university placed a hold on his registration until he could pay back the tuition he owed for the previous two quarters—a sum of several thousand dollars. Sergio did not have the money to pay his son's debt. "We have to work," he told Jorge. "You're only going to be out of school for a year."

It was almost five years before Jorge returned to UC Riverside in the fall of 2014. Newly admitted for the second time, Jorge's experience was different. As a DACA recipient, he had temporary legal status and a work permit, which would make it easier for him to find employment on or near campus. Though he was still not eligible for federal financial aid, the new California

DREAM Act opened state grants and private scholarships to undocumented students so he could more easily cover the expenses of college. Jorge also had a new course of study. He would be majoring in public policy.

I met Jorge at the National Summit on Undocumented Students sponsored by the UC Office of the President in the spring of 2015.

Jorge received the invitation to apply to be a student representative in April. It was near the end of his first year back at UC Riverside, and he had chosen to focus more on his studies than on extracurricular activities. However, because of his new major in public policy, Jorge thought that the summit would be a good opportunity for him to learn about education policy related to immigrant students. He did not anticipate that, on the evening he arrived, he would be planning a protest alongside other undocumented UC students.

Jorge spoke on one of the panels that students organized after they took over the summit. I knew that he was a representative from Riverside, but I hadn't met him yet. As I watched him on the stage that afternoon, I could see that he was listening attentively to his peers. When he finally spoke, his ideas and opinions were thoughtful and undergirded by quiet confidence. I learned later that he had gone to the summit to learn about education policy but instead he found himself teaching others about the needs of undocumented students and what kind of university policies would be needed to truly support them.

When I talked to him about his experience as an undocumented student advocate, he told me that the UC Undocumented Student Summit had been a turning point for him. It made him understand that he was not alone. Listening to the student activists there and learning about the work that they had been doing even before the summit had inspired and energized him. He felt as if his own college experience had been a "horror story," but for some reason he had survived it. Though he had met some undocumented students at UC Riverside who shared his experiences through PODER, he realized during the week of the summit in Oakland that there were probably hundreds more students across California who had experienced migration trauma and were still trying to move forward. If he could make it, so could they, and he could help them. He could inspire them by his presence, but he could also teach them the lessons he had learned about how the immigration and education systems work. On a broader level, Jorge realized that he could also help to advocate for policy changes.

Jorge's horror story was the result of the stark differences in the way that policies are formulated for migrants deemed deserving or undeserving of humane treatment. While Jorge was struggling through college, a certain cross-section of politicians in Washington supported the DREAM Act because they determined that migrants such as Jorge were deserving of citizenship. At the same time, the number of migrant deaths in the Arizona desert were rising because of border-militarization policies that aimed to keep undeserving migrants out of the country. Jorge's experience poignantly illustrates that the line between so-called deserving and undeserving immigrants is permeable, if not altogether false. In his case, the "undeserving" migrant who almost lost his life crossing the desert was his father. Over the days that he had no news of Sergio's whereabouts, Jorge learned and felt the ramification of years of border-militarization policy. Though not intended to affect his life as a college student, draconian policing of the border, because of the intimate connections between father and son, rendered both of them vulnerable and ultimately punished by it.

When Jorge returned to UC Riverside, he knew that public policy would be a course of study that would resonate with him, especially immigration policy. As he became involved with the UC Undocumented Student Coalition, he realized that he already had a deep understanding of such policies because of his lived experience.[43] Though what he had learned had largely been "undocumented," he was able to bring that knowledge to bear in the classroom and in his advocacy work.

2

UNDOCUMENTED PEDAGOGIES OF HOME

Jazmin remembers hard summer rain in her ranchito in Guanajuato during the few days that she had to prepare to migrate to the United States. The warm rain came down in sheets, rattling tin rooftops and settling the dust in town, packing it into hard mud. She was twelve years old, and for the previous seven months Jazmin had been living apart from her parents and younger sister. Her mother and sister had migrated to the United States after three years of separation from Jazmin's father. He had been migrating from Guanajuato to California since Jazmin was born in the mid-1990s, and though the money he sent to his family every month helped them to stay afloat, the long separations were beginning to wear on all of them. The family did not have enough to pay a coyote to cross Jazmin's mother and her two daughters at once, so they decided to cross in stages; they would send for Jazmin when they had saved enough money.

The summer of rain accelerated their plans.

Jazmin's paternal grandfather arrived to visit his son who was ill, and the family with whom Jazmin was staying decided that it would be an opportune time to send the teenager north when he made the return trip. Her grandfather could take her as far as Tijuana and then make arrangements for her to cross. Jazmin's family waited until the day before to tell her that she would be going with him. Surprised but resigned, Jazmin agreed to go even on such short notice.[1] She wasn't sure what to pack. After a quick phone call to her mother, she decided on her birth certificate, her sixth-grade graduation certificate, one hundred pesos (the equivalent of about $10), and one change of clothes. She wanted to say goodbye to her friends. But the rain made everything more difficult. She left saying goodbye only to her maternal grandparents and made her way with her paternal grandfather to the border.

Jazmin understood that her father's absences were tied to her family's economic security. She was told that before he started to work in the United States, her family did not have enough money to buy basic necessities to live. She knew they were facing the kind of poverty that would leave them hungry. Jazmin expected that things would be better in the United States, and in some ways they were better. Once they were all reunited, her family settled and was working in an affluent city on the central coast of California. The city was pristine, its downtown buildings white with red Spanish-tiled rooftops. The weather was always temperate—warm in the day and cool in the mornings and evenings. The sun always shone, and the sky was always clear. Jazmin could see the blue line of the ocean along the horizon from different vantage points in the city; the faint scent of salt was always in the air. Though this was lovely, Jazmin was always aware of the sharp divide between the families who lived in the expansive homes with coastal views and those immigrant families like her own, who lived either in cramped apartments or in crowded houses with multiple families. She also knew that their labor facilitated the lives of these wealthy coastal residents. They were nannies and landscapers, cooks and house cleaners. Many were also undocumented migrants from Latin American countries, and most of them lived in poverty.

Jazmin's parents were part of what Patricia Zavella refers to as "the working poor": those who work full time or for significant amounts of time in one job or more, yet still fall below the poverty line.[2] Her father worked for a landscaping company, and her mother worked in restaurants and as a hotel maid. As a young teenager, Jazmin couldn't help but notice the effect that her parents' labor had on their bodies. Her mother had a job making tortillas at a restaurant, rolling them out, tossing them onto a hot comal, grabbing and flipping them with her bare hands. She would come home with burn marks on her fingers that eventually became small scars before she transitioned to a job as a hotel maid. Similarly, Jazmin remembers being surprised by the roughness of her father's hands. They reminded her of her grandmother in Guanajuato, whose hands were rough from chopping wood, feeding animals, and harvesting maíz and beans on the family farm. While her grandmother was elderly, Jazmin's father was just forty. She thought, *He suffered in Mexico; why does he have to suffer here, too?*

The summer that Jazmin arrived in the United States, she would join her mother in English classes at the local adult school after she returned from her shift at the restaurant. Nevertheless, when it was time for Jazmin to begin junior high school that August, the school wanted to place her in the local elementary school because of her limited English skills. Jazmin's mother fought for her daughter to be placed in her appropriate grade. She had just finished elementary school in Guanajuato, and her mother knew that she was prepared for the next level. In fact, Jazmin's mother asked her daughter to pack her sixth-grade graduation certificate among the few items she brought to the United States. Anticipating that the school would want Jazmin to repeat sixth grade because of her emerging English-language proficiency, she wanted to ensure that her daughter would be enrolled in seventh grade.[3] Ultimately, the junior high school allowed Jazmin to register, and she decided to put all of her energy into learning English.

Jazmin listened to music in English; she watched cartoons and her favorite movies—dubbed in Spanish for Mexican television—in their original English. She watched music videos and commentary on MTV. Her younger sister, who was in kindergarten, had a compact disc from school that they listened to together. She learned "The ABC Song," the rhymes "Humpty Dumpty" and "Hey Diddle," and a song about colors. Jazmin read board books with simple English words and phrases, and slowly she was able to read her sister's homework. Although they were seven years apart in age, the two of them were learning English together. Jazmin was thirteen, but she made no friends. She was not involved in school clubs; she never went out. Her full-time occupation was to learn English.

Family and Undocumented Education

Jazmin's life story dramatically illustrates a young person's awareness of poverty and labor exploitation within the context of her undocumented immigrant family. Her parents made the calculated decision that it was better to be poor in the United States than to be poor in Mexico. They worked not only for economic survival, but also—as Jazmin's mother's advocacy at the school indicates—for their children to have educational and economic opportunities. In this chapter, I examine how such parental decisions and working-class work ethics can provide an educational and activist framework for undocumented children. Through their labor and advocacy, undocumented parents can teach their children an ethic of hard work through example. Underlying such lessons are implicit and sometimes explicit lessons about class exploitation.[4] In addition to these working-class pedagogies of home, migrant parents teach their children how to navigate their undocumented legal status, including advocacy. Class and legal status are intertwined for many undocumented families, but the lessons parents teach about illegality are often distinct. These lessons might include how to stay safe when faced with law enforcement or what rights are available to them. I am also interested in the soft lessons that parents teach their children; soft skills can include resilience/endurance and hope. This chapter focuses on how some undocumented youth were able to build on their families' undocumented pedagogies of home to move through the kindergarten–college educational pipeline and, ultimately, into advocacy work.

Centering the learning that occurs in the homes of migrant families is important because it demonstrates the deep connections between undocumented young people and their parents. An analysis of these undocumented pedagogies of home also helps us understand how the knowledge students glean from their families can prepare them for higher education. The stories in this chapter illustrate how pedagogies of home plant seeds for educational success, as well as civic engagement and community activism. To frame this discussion, I rely on the Chicana feminist education scholar Dolores Delgado Bernal's conception of pedagogies of the home, which she defines as "the communication, practices, and learning that occur in the home and community . . . [that] serve as a cultural knowledge base that helps Chicana college students negotiate the daily experiences of sexist, racist, and classist microaggressions."[5] Undocumented parents also provide their children with a "knowledge base" that helps them to navigate higher education. While undocumented college students often experience the same types of microaggressions, they must also contend with anti-immigrant rhetoric in classroom spaces, which ranges from unintentionally to intentionally hostile. For example, a classmate might blithely refer to undocumented workers as "illegals" during an in-class discussion or a professor might extemporaneously assert that immigrants are bad for the California economy. The 2016 presidential election heightened such rhetoric. Students not only heard anti-immigrant messages from political pundits, but cross-sections of social media and some of their peers became emboldened to espouse anti-immigrant messages. Strong undocumented pedagogies of home help undocumented young people to know differently. Students know their parents' work ethics and are aware of labor exploitation and thus understand how immigrants contribute to the economy. They might also have had a sense of dignity instilled in their homes to know that no human being is illegal.

I also consider how this home-based knowledge serves as a form of cultural capital that helps undocumented students navigate their paths through college and give back to their communities through advocacy and activism. Tara Yosso's model of community cultural wealth is helpful to understand this unique cultural capital. Yosso identifies forms of "capital" apart from money and material resources, including cultural, linguistic, resistant, navigational, social, familial, and aspirational capital.[6] Taken together, she argues, these form the basis of community cultural wealth. Undocumented parents and families can similarly provide their children with these types of cultural assets.

Pedagogies of home and community cultural wealth do not exist in a vacuum. For as much as parents might encourage children to work hard and instill values that lead to resilience and hope, such lessons are constrained by the social, political, and economic conditions of the outside world. Undocumented legal status affects families' ability to find stable and well-paying jobs. It constrains mobility.[7] Furthermore, while parents might teach their children positive values, attitudes, and skills, they also impart their anxieties.[8] Nevertheless, the undocumented young people in this chapter were able to take their families' pedagogies of home and navigate the constraints of their illegality to matriculate in college. Some of their paths were circuitous, and no one entered the university without feeling the structural constraints and emotional impact of their legal status.

Most of the young people in my study found out that they were undocumented only when they were nearing the end of high school and preparing to apply to college. In these cases, parents had to help their children approach the system of higher education without the same rights as young people who were citizens. In fewer cases, parents raised their children with the knowledge that they were in the country without legal authorization. In these scenarios, parents explicitly taught their children how to stay safe when driving, for example, and what to do if they were pulled over by a US Border Patrol agent. I argue that pedagogies of home occur both implicitly and explicitly and are just as important as the education that undocumented young people receive in school, because they represent not only knowledge, but also critical consciousness. This kind of consciousness includes critical awareness of class exploitation or discrimination on the basis of immigration status, race, gender, ability, or any intersection of these identities. For some, this consciousness is well developed at an early age through experiences at home and in communities. For others, it is an emerging consciousness that begins at home but is more fully realized in college settings.

In this chapter I argue that parents' undocumented pedagogies of home teach work ethics, build class consciousness, and inform children how to navigate illegality. All of this can bolster undocumented Latinx students' feelings of belonging and even their academic performance in formal spaces of education. This is to say that undocumented *parents* are key figures and influences in the academic success of their children—so-called Dreamers. Furthermore, the cultural wealth that undocumented young people gain from their families, coupled with the critical consciousness that emerges at home and in school spaces, is an integral part of their political formation and their advocacy on behalf of the larger undocumented community. It is this kind of multifaceted education that motivates students to work toward what they perceive to be a more just society.

Learning to Labor

The 2008 recession deeply affected Jazmin's family. Her father lost his job with the landscaping company. He and some friends decided to borrow money for another business venture, but when that failed, the family was left with debt. Then, in 2009, Jazmin's younger brother was born. Taking stock of their assets and expenses, Jazmin's parents once again decided to relocate. This time they would move to Fresno, where the family could live with Jazmin's grandparents in a less expensive region of California until the family found their economic footing again.

Fresno is in the heart of the Central Valley of California, a region with a highly developed and productive agricultural industry that yields much of the produce that feeds the rest of the country. For most of the twentieth century to today, that industry has depended on immigrant labor. For twenty of those years, the valley's agriculture industry was bolstered by *bracero* labor—a contract guest worker program between the United States and Mexico that undercut union organizing and kept wages low and working conditions poor. After the end of the Bracero Program in 1965, Mexican and Filipino farmworkers organized the United Farm Workers of America (UFW), which helped to shine a national spotlight on the exploitative working conditions of farmworkers in the Central Valley.[9] While the UFW made important gains in the 1960s and 1970s, wages and working conditions for farmworkers in the Central Valley continue to be less than desirable. During peak harvest season in the summer, temperatures soar upward of 100 degrees Fahrenheit, and the work itself is physically taxing. Nevertheless, agriculture continues to be the primary field of labor available to migrants in that region.

Jazmin quickly realized that her family would have limited work options when they moved to Fresno. She joined her parents and grandfather picking table grapes the summer before her first year of high school. They would arrive at the farm at 6 a.m. to begin work before the sun fully bore down on the fields. Jazmin emulated the other workers, dressing in long-sleeved men's shirts, old jeans, a hat, and a kerchief to protect her face from dust. She made her way down the rows of grapes as quickly as she could, but as a novice farmworker she made mistakes. Jazmin injured herself with the knife that she was using to remove the heavy bundles of grapes from the vine. Her dust-covered wound emanated pain though her left hand, but she knew that she had to continue to make her hours in the fields worth something. They were working for a farm that paid a piece rate, which meant that the grower paid based on the weight of what the worker had picked rather than the time that she worked. Even though she might work eleven-hour days, Jazmin was paid only by the weight of what she picked. School began, and Jazmin worked afternoons with her grandfather while her mother worked in the packing sheds. Their job at the farm ended when the vines were empty and the green leaves that draped from the vines began to change color to orange, red, and brown. It was fall, and Jazmin's family had to find work at another farm with a later harvest season to continue to earn a living. Knowing that this type of work was not sustainable, Jazmin's father returned to the coast to look for another job.

Jazmin, her mother, and her grandfather transitioned to another farm, picking green beans in the late fall and early winter. They returned to the grape vineyards to prune and prepare for the harvest the following summer. At the predominantly Latino high school Jazmin attended, her work situation was not unique. Her classmates also worked in the fields after school, all of them doing their part to contribute to the economic stability of their families.[10] Jazmin finished work in the vineyards and returned the following summer for another season of grapes. At the end of the summer, Jazmin's father felt that he had a good enough job for all of them to return to the coast. Though the pay was not high, the job was more stable than field work, and he would be paid hourly rather than by piece.

Even with greater economic stability, Jazmin and her family continued to live in poverty. During her last three years of high school, Jazmin and her family changed houses and apartments no fewer than three times. When they first returned from Fresno, her family rented a room in a house with seven other families. Jazmin would remember this as the worst home she would ever live in. The bathroom never seemed to be empty. She would have to wake at one or two in the morning to shower before school. The kitchen, likewise, was always crowded. Her family bought a camp stove so they could prepare food and eat outside. Jazmin would rush home after school to relieve the babysitter and care for her baby brother because, even though both of her parents were working and they were living in a house shared with other people, the cost of the babysitter was a strain.[11] Again, she had no school friends, and she never went out. Her job was to cook for the family, clean their space in the house, and care for her younger siblings while her mother and father worked. Jazmin was still a teenager, but at some level she understood that her labor at home was a piece of her family's financial puzzle. She recognized how hard they worked at their jobs, and she tried to emulate that work ethic at home.

Remarkably, and despite her family's economic stresses, Jazmin excelled at school. She applied the same work ethic that she learned to keep her family afloat to her schoolwork. Jazmin joined the Advancement via Individual Determination (AVID) program at her high school and a pathway program connected to the local university. The AVID program taught her skills such as taking notes in class and using them to study; it also laid out the path to attend a four-year university, ensuring that she would meet high school curricular requirements. In AVID she found mentors who advised her on how to navigate the educational system and her status as an undocumented person within that system. She attended events at the local university and made connections with other undocumented young people who were already in college. These young people also became mentors who advised her about how to imagine a college life as an undocumented person. Perhaps most important, they were proof that, even without papers, she could go to college. By the end of high school, Jazmin was enrolled in advanced placement classes. Though she still struggled with English, she had an affinity and gift for math, so she decided to apply to college as an applied mathematics major.

Jazmin was accepted to several colleges and universities in the spring of 2013. She was thrilled and relieved that her work to learn English and to prioritize school in the face of her family's economic hardships had paid off. These feelings were quickly replaced by anxiety as Jazmin and her family faced a difficult decision. Jazmin aspired to attend one of the University of California (UC) campuses that had offered her admission. Riverside had offered her the most robust financial aid package, a combination of funding from the California Development, Relief, and Education for Alien Minors (DREAM) Act and university resources; however, the UC Riverside campus was significantly closer to the US-Mexico border than where her family lived. Jazmin's father was nervous that she would be vulnerable to deportation at a campus in Southern California. His fears were not unfounded. A Border Patrol field office was located less than two miles from the UC Riverside campus from 1967 until 2012.[12] While that office was closed during the Obama administration, Riverside County remained part of the El Centro Sector of the US Border Patrol.

To assuage her father's concerns, Jazmin decided to consult an immigration attorney about her status. Less than a year before, in August 2012, the Obama administration had enacted Deferred Action for Childhood Arrivals (DACA) as a temporary legal protection for undocumented youth who had been brought to the United States by their parents. She thought that she might qualify for the program, but she also knew that she had arrived in the United States just weeks before the eligibility cutoff date of June 15, 2007. Unfortunately, because Jazmin did not enter school until late August, the lawyer determined that she did not have sufficient proof of continuous residency to qualify for DACA. Jazmin was devastated. Not only would she not have the legal protections of DACA; she would also be ineligible for the policy's two-year work permit that would have enabled her to work and help pay her way through college. She was eighteen, and she was scared to move to a place within immediate reach of Immigration and Customs Enforcement (ICE).

Jazmin thought about all of her family's migrations and moves, the many jobs and terrible working and living conditions. She considered her own sacrifice of a social life to take care of her younger siblings, her struggles to learn English, and the long hours she had invested studying and learning about the US education system. Jazmin knew that a college degree would benefit not only her but also her family. She could have a stable job that would not require backbreaking work and would pay a living wage. She thought about how her parents had left their home and traveled to another country at great risk to provide a better life for her family; this was often what motivated her to work so diligently in school and to contribute to the household labor. She would only be a four-hour drive from her home, and the promise of a college education would be worth it not only for her, but for all of them. She decided that she would have to risk it. Jazmin applied for as many scholarships as she could to supplement the university's financial aid package. She reached out to her connections at the local university for advice, and they placed her in contact with the leaders of Providing Opportunities, Dreams, and Education in Riverside (PODER).

Jazmin's first two quarters at Riverside were difficult as she built her social support system at the university. Perhaps most acutely she felt the stress of her strained finances as she struggled to cover the expenses of moving to an apartment; tuition and fees; and the astronomical price of textbooks, which could cost up to $300 each if purchased brand new. By her second quarter, Jazmin was unsure how she was going to continue to pay rent, as her parents could not help her. She connected with Estella Acuña, the director of the office of Chicano Student Programs, who pointed her to additional scholarships to help bridge the gap in her budget.[13] She wrote scholarship essays in addition to her regular coursework. Though she was attending PODER meetings, it was taking time to feel like she belonged to the already tight-knit group of students in the group. Slowly, Jazmin began to cultivate friendships unlike any she had had before. These were students who, like her, understood what it was like to live as an undocumented person. They had similar financial struggles and anxieties about deportation (if not for themselves, for their parents). However, the other thing they had in common was the desire to create a space for undocumented students to feel safe on campus and to create pathways for high school students to attend UC Riverside, as well.

The friendships that Jazmin formed in PODER would ultimately support her when she began to feel waves of depression and insecurity about her migration; her family's economic struggles; and her experiences of illegality. When she felt as if she did not belong, as if she should not be at the university, her friends in PODER understood and offered her support and encouragement. They would tell her, "Come on. Don't give up. You can do it." After so many years of having no social life and few meaningful friend-ships, Jazmin found a new family among the other members of PODER. They were similarly motivated to work hard—this time, the labor was in school, for their communities, and especially at this juncture, for one another.[14]

Jazmin's parents modeled a deep work ethic for the economic survival of their family. Jazmin's own work ethic mirrored that of her parents, es-pecially in her academic work. The latter was, on one hand, to make her parents' sacrifices worthwhile. On the other hand, Jazmin believed that aca-demic work, ultimately resulting in a college degree, would help to lift her family out of poverty. Once she was in college, however, Jazmin felt some of the limits of hard work. Like her parents, who worked relentlessly but could not make their way out of poverty, she was beginning to see more clearly the structures that were limiting her ability to focus on her college education: the financial aid policies, her inability to access DACA, the im-migration policies that continued to constrain her parents' lives (and thus her own). Jazmin's next lessons would be about community and advocacy through her involvement in PODER.

Learning to Be Illegal

Alejandro does not recall a time when he did not know about his undocu-mented legal status. His parents migrated from Michoacán, Mexico, to the United States in the 1970s, a time period scholars identify as the begin-ning of a contemporary large-scale migration. Though their community of Uruápan was flanked by avocado and macadamia orchards and had an active agricultural economy, Mexico's high levels of unemployment and popula-tion growth spurred both documented and undocumented migration to the United States.[15] Alejandro's parents settled in a community east of Los Angeles and began to make a life there. His father aspired to find a job that provided enough so that his wife did not have to work, and initially that was possible. When Alejandro's two older siblings were born in the early 1980s, his mother was able to stay home to care for them. After almost a decade in the United States, a family emergency compelled Alejandro's parents to return to Michoacán to care for his maternal grandmother. It was during that time in Mexico that Alejandro was born.

When their family situation stabilized, Alejandro's parents made plans to return to the United States. They both had legal documents that would enable them to return, and because Alejandro's older siblings were born in the United States, their citizenship enabled them to travel freely into the country. Alejandro—who was only nine months old—was the only member of the family who would have to cross without papers. Using the birth certificate of a family friend who had a baby born in Los Angeles, Alejandro's aunt carried him in her arms across the border.

Despite their belief that they would have greater economic security in the United States, the economic recession of the 1990s meant that Alejandro's parents would struggle to find their footing again in Los Angeles. They could not afford an apartment, so the family of five lived in a converted garage until Alejandro was four years old. Even though he was young, Alejandro would always remember Los Angeles as crowded, with little space to move. When his mother became pregnant, the family decided to look for another city to call home.

Alejandro's parents heard that housing was more affordable in San Bernardino. Though only fifty miles east of Los Angeles, it might as well have been a different world. Settlement in the Inland Empire, the region of Southern California that includes San Bernardino, dramatically increased after World War II. The postwar period marked a "profound demographic and economic transformation" for the region bolstered by blue-collar jobs at the Kaiser Steel mill in Fontana, at Norton Air Force Base, and with the Santa Fe Railroad.[16] When those industries shuttered and moved away in the 1980s and 1990s, so did many white, working middle-class residents.[17] Despite the economic downturn spurred by the loss of union and government jobs, the population of San Bernardino grew almost 40 percent in the 1980s. The new settlers were often refugees from Los Angeles, immigrants and people of color looking for affordable housing and a break from the congestion of urban life. By the early 1990s, nearly half the population was Latino; about 20 percent were Black; and about 30 percent of the city was White.[18] Media representation of San Bernardino during that time period focused on how initiatives by the Los Angeles Police Department pushed gangs east toward the Inland Empire and high rates of crime.[19] However, for many working-class families, San Bernardino in the 1990s was a "place to start over, build families and get working-class jobs."[20] For Mexican immigrant families, it was a place where they could frequent swap meets to purchase or barter for home goods and where they could find Mexican treats from vendors pushing carts in their neighborhoods. There was crime, yes, but there was also community. Moreover, because the city was still flanked by the fields of a slowly waning agricultural economy, it felt like there was more space in San Bernardino, more room to breathe.

It was in this complex and growing area that Alejandro's parents raised their young family. His father found a job relatively quickly with a construction company, and the family moved into a two-bedroom house in the northwestern corner of San Bernardino. Though the area of town was working class and sometimes marked by gang violence, the house was on a corner lot with a large backyard, where Alejandro and his siblings could play under and around the shade trees. Alejandro's mother, who stayed at home—partly because of the scarcity of jobs and partly because her husband wanted her to focus on her domestic role—found ways to supplement her husband's income. She sold sweet and sticky *raspados* out of the family garage to the neighborhood kids and Avon and Mary Kay products to other women on the block. Other families knew and respected her so much that gangs were careful to leave Alejandro's house out of the crosshairs when altercations arose.

Alejandro began kindergarten at a public elementary school half a mile down the street from his house, where he made friends with other Latinx and Black children from working-class families. He picked up English quickly, but school never interested him. Even though his parents would say, "Tú eres el que naciste en Mexico" (You were the one born in Mexico), Alejandro considered himself a normal American child. There was something pointed in the way they would remind him about his nativity, and Alejandro knew it was significant, but not to its full extent. He would even tell his friends, *I'm from Mexico*, without entirely understanding that he was an *undocumented* person from Mexico.

By junior high, Alejandro was working with his father for a construction company, helping to put final touches on model homes. He swept streets, cleaned paint that dripped onto staged furniture or windows, and performed small repairs that the houses needed. On the site, he was his dad's apprentice. Because he shared a name with his father, the company bosses referred to him as "little Alex." Alejandro didn't mind the work because everyone in his family worked. He always thought, however, that when he was old enough he would get a work permit, a driver's license, and a better job. He imagined a job at the mall where his friends would hang out rather than working under the watchful eye of his father. It was precisely when he was nearing the end of high school, old enough to apply for a driver's license and for jobs at the mall, that he began to understand the implications of his legal status. Because he didn't have a Social Security number, he couldn't take the driver's license exam.[21] He wasn't able to walk into a chain store at the mall and fill out a job application. Determined to find a job on his own, Alejandro began to ask friends and family about jobs for which he might be eligible. He began to find work in mom-and-pop restaurants that paid him in cash and off the books. His first job was at a Mongolian barbecue restaurant, where he learned how to prepare meat and vegetables and to cook on a scorching circular cast iron grill.

By the time Alejandro was in high school, his parents had saved enough money to buy a house on the south side of San Bernardino. Alejandro graduated from high school and looked for better jobs, and he began to work more hours. Almost all of these jobs were for family-owned restaurants that paid him in cash. He worked to pay his bills and to help his family. His earnings also paid tuition at the local community college where he had enrolled. Alejandro wasn't sure yet about college or a career, but he thought community college was a good place to start.

For a few years, Alejandro managed his work, social, and school life by catching rides with his family, riding his bicycle, or walking. However, when his family bought a house in nearby Rialto in 2007, Alejandro felt that he had no choice but to buy a car of his own. With cash that he had saved from his jobs, Alejandro went to a local used car dealership in a neighboring city and purchased a four-year-old black Ford Focus. The two-door hatchback had a manual transmission, and Alejandro did not yet know how to drive a stick shift, but the price was within his budget, and the car would provide a way for him to traverse the city. Alejandro's parents did not feel comfortable with him driving not only without a license, but also without legal authorization to be in the country. Nevertheless, they knew that he was an adult who needed to move around the region independently. "We can't restrict you," they said, which he took as their permission.

Though his parents had always reminded Alejandro that he was born in Mexico, their messages to him now had more urgency. They feared that even a routine traffic stop might have profound consequences. Police checkpoints to crack down on drunk drivers emerged in the 1990s and appeared with greater frequency in the region through the 2000s. Though these traffic stops were ostensibly intended to identify people who were driving under the influence, the police were also citing and impounding the cars of people who were driving without licenses—for example, unauthorized migrants.[22] Alejandro's parents' anxieties were augmented by reports they would hear on television about the presence of ICE officers in their community. In 2005, the year Alejandro turned eighteen, San Bernardino County entered into a memorandum of understanding (MOU) with ICE that allowed local law enforcement to be trained and deputized to enforce federal immigration law.[23] The following year, Riverside, the county directly south of San Bernardino, also entered into an MOU with ICE, ostensibly to protect Riverside County from "criminal" immigrants.[24] These new local immigration policies added to the US Border Patrol presence in the region. The intensification of policing and patrolling of undocumented immigrants in the Inland Empire during the mid-2000s increased Alejandro's family's anxieties about deportation.

Alejandro's parents lived with that worry, comforting themselves with the hope that they had taught him enough to be safe when driving. For his part, Alejandro lived with the confidence of an invincible teenager. He was frustrated by his inability to find work and to secure a driver's license in the "normal" way, but he didn't feel the same fear his parents did. Logically, he understood that he was undocumented, but he didn't feel any different from his siblings. He tried to heed their warnings. He conditioned himself to be vigilant of law enforcement, always checking his rearview mirror for California Highway Patrol or Border Patrol. Alejandro did receive traffic tickets, and at one point his car was impounded, but to his parents' relief he was never detained for deportation proceedings.

Instead, Alejandro continued to work in different jobs while taking courses at the local community college. After seven years, he earned an associate's degree in liberal studies. It was 2012, and in another month President Barack Obama would announce the DACA program. News of DACA ran through the Latinx community in San Bernardino. Seeing DACA as an opportunity for their son, Alejandro's parents encouraged him to apply. "You have to do this," they would tell him. But Alejandro was hesitant. The application fee was more than $400, and he did not have that money on hand. More than that, however, he did not know whether DACA was a legitimate program or whether he would even be eligible. By that point, he had heard that several people had applied and been rejected, and Alejandro had an arrest on his record. Finally, his parents convinced him to consult with a *notario*, who would charge $275 to help him fill out the application.[25] The *notario* was encouraging, noting that because Alejandro's arrest was for a misdemeanor, it was not likely to affect his case. The charge was included in his DACA application, and by February 2013 Alejandro had received his DACA documentation in the mail.

Rather than relief, Alejandro felt anger as he parsed through the documentation. He thought, *Four hundred dollars for this piece of shit just so I can be considered somewhat legal?* He didn't know where the anger came from, but it was there. He looked over the materials, put them on his desk at home, and resumed his normal life. A week later, Alejandro's parents, having given him time to feel angry, said, "OK. You have to go take the test for your driver's license."

Though he passed the driving portion of test on his first try, it took him a few attempts to pass the written portion. The night he passed, Alejandro went out to celebrate with his best friend. At twenty-five, he finally had a driver's license. Alejandro promised himself that he would never work at another restaurant again. This was a promise that he could not keep for long. When a friend offered him a job working at a restaurant inside a local mall, he had to say yes because he needed the work. He finally had that job at the mall he had wanted as a teenager, but now he was the old guy in the work crew. This was still not the life that he wanted for himself.

Alejandro's parents had always encouraged him to go to school, but earning his associate's degree was not opening the doors they thought it would, even with DACA. He decided to return to the community college to see what other options he could find. The second time around, Alejandro met two other undocumented students. He finally had people in his life he could talk to about his status. They shared their experiences with one another, including how they managed to navigate school and work without papers. Hearing their stories and reflecting on his own journey made him realize everything he had gone through to get to that point in his life, and he felt empowered. He had come this far with little academic guidance or support. While his parents could encourage him to continue his studies, they could not teach him how to navigate the school system. With fresh eyes he saw what he had not been able to see as a teenager: all the ways he might have slipped through the cracks; how helpful it might have been to have a teacher or a counselor to offer him understanding and academic support. He decided that he was going to take classes at the community college to transfer to a four-year university, and he was going to become a teacher. In the fall of 2014, he matriculated at UC Riverside.

Learning to Advocate

Mafalda was born with a floating spine.[26] He had a condition called sacral agenesis, which meant, among other things, that he was missing the lower part of his spine—three vertebrae and a tailbone.[27] Doctors in Guadalajara, Mexico, where Mafalda and his twin brother were born, determined that Mafalda would never be able to walk or even sit up; he would spend his entire life lying down. Mafalda's parents, Yolanda and Antonio, were devastated. When the initial shock of the diagnosis faded, however, they began to look for second opinions and solutions. It was 1994, and they lived in one of the biggest metropolitan areas in Mexico, second only to Mexico City; they believed that there had to be other options. During the first several months of Mafalda's life, Yolanda and Antonio paid thousands of dollars to specialists in and around Guadalajara, but none of them could give them any answers. Then Yolanda's sister, who lived in the United States, found out about a children's hospital that specialized in orthopedics and spinal cord injuries: Shriners Hospital for Children in Los Angeles. Mafalda's parents scheduled an appointment and traveled with him to the United States for a consultation.

The doctors at Shriners Hospital offered Yolanda and Antonio hope. Though there wouldn't be a single solution, a series of surgeries would help Mafalda's mobility and strength. Medical specialists proposed multiple operations, recovery periods, and follow-up visits during his early childhood development. Periodic procedures would be necessary as long as Mafalda's bones continued to grow. While such a course of treatment seemed daunting, the expense was not: they learned that Shriners Hospitals offered medical services free of charge to children up to the age of eighteen, regardless of a family's immigration status. When they understood the scope of the proposed treatment and realized that the hospital offered affordable access to care that was not available in their home country, Yolanda and Antonio knew they would need to move their small family to Los Angeles.

They were a young married couple starting their life together. Yolanda worked for a Mexican airline, and Antonio worked at a travel agency; they had a stable middle-class life in Guadalajara. They used their airline benefits to travel across the country and into the United States to see their favorite bands in concert—Soda Stereo in Mexico City, U2 in Miami. They owned a home. The priority now, however, was to do whatever they could so that Mafalda could gain enough mobility to enjoy his life. The couple quit their jobs, sold their home, and moved to the Inland Empire, east of Los Angeles, where they could be near family and within driving distance of the hospital. Mafalda and his twin brother were one year old.

Yolanda immediately found work cleaning houses, and Antonio eventually found a job at a travel agency. They struggled to adjust to their new lives in Southern California. Once middle-class professionals, they were now working-class migrants. Though they both spoke some English, it was not their dominant language. Exacerbating matters was the upsurge of a hostile climate for immigrants in California, fostered by Governor Pete Wilson. When Yolanda and Antonio first arrived in Los Angeles for their consultation with the Shriners doctors, Wilson had recently been reelected on a strongly anti-immigrant platform. A key part of that was his support for Proposition 187, the so-called Save Our State initiative, which would have denied unauthorized immigrants access to non-emergency health care and public education, among other services.[28] Fortunately for Yolanda and Antonio, that law would have applied only to hospitals that received state funding; Shriners did not. Though the proposition itself was ultimately found to be unconstitutional, Latino advocacy groups noted an upsurge in anti-Latino violence and aggression in the months following the 1994 election, when voters passed Proposition 187.[29] It was in this political climate that Yolanda and Antonio unsuccessfully attempted to extend their family's tourist visas and petition for legal permanent residency.

Meanwhile, Mafalda was receiving the medical care that they had hoped for. Against the initial prognosis they received from doctors in Mexico, Mafalda had taken his first steps by the time he was three. Yolanda and Antonio were determined to see how far the course of treatment at Shriners could take their child. When their tourist visas expired, they decided to stay in Los Angeles, and Yolanda, Antonio, Mafalda, and his twin became undocumented.

Over the next several years, Yolanda was able to capitalize on her education in Mexico to find a white-collar job and began work as an accountant for a chain of Mexican grocery stores. Antonio's steadiest work was as a newspaper carrier, which he was able to supplement from time to time with other part-time jobs. When Mafalda was old enough to go to school, they decided to enroll him in a school for children with disabilities. In this context they could be certain that teachers and staff would be able to support Mafalda's academic development and his unique physiological needs. After two years, Yolanda and Antonio decided that Mafalda was ready to attend a mainstream school. Though Mafalda would still need some physical assistance, his parents wanted him to begin to develop social and navigational skills that would help him lead an independent life.

The transition was difficult. While teachers and staff at the first school were specially trained to support children with disabilities, staff and faculty at the new school were untrained and sometimes unwilling to help Mafalda, even when he could articulate exactly what he needed. Yolanda was a constant fixture at the school, advocating for her child. She took her concerns to the principal, and when the principal was unresponsive, she went to the superintendent. She made sure that teachers and the school nurse knew how to manage Mafalda's situation. Guided by an awareness that schools might dismiss her child's needs because he came from an immigrant family, Yolanda was almost aggressive in her approach. She had left her life behind in Mexico to save her child's life; she was not going to leave Mafalda's education to chance. It was precisely this desire that led Yolanda and Antonio, when Mafalda was poised to enter high school, to enroll him at International Polytechnic High School (iPoly) in Pomona, California.

Though it was a public school, iPoly operated almost like a private school, maintaining a small size—about five hundred students in the entire high school—and an innovative curriculum, which it characterized as entirely "college prep." The school did not charge tuition, but students had to pass an entrance exam and meet a grade point average (GPA) requirement to enroll. Mafalda easily met the admissions requirements and genuinely felt a sense of belonging at the school, as a person with a disability from an immigrant background and, ultimately, as someone who identified as queer. While Yolanda and Antonio were happy that Mafalda was doing well both academically and socially at iPoly, what was particularly appealing was iPoly's offering of dual college enrollment for junior and senior students who met certain academic standards during their freshman and sophomore years. If all went well, Mafalda would be able to earn college credit during high school without the family incurring the expense of college tuition.

At the end of Mafalda's sophomore year of high school, the life that Yolanda and Antonio had vigilantly and carefully created for their family began to fall apart. It was the spring of 2010, and growing hostility toward migrants precipitated Governor Jan Brewer's signing of Arizona Senate Bill (SB) 1070 into law. The law made residing or working in the United States without legal permission an Arizona state crime; required law enforcement officers to verify the legal status of any person who was arrested or detained in the state; and allowed officers to arrest people without a warrant based on probable cause of unlawful presence.[30] The law caused an uproar, renewing a national debate about the immigration "problem." This Arizona law was significant to Mafalda's family because Yolanda was employed by a chain of Mexican grocery stores that was based in Arizona. When the law passed, the owner of the chain was compelled to fire all of his undocumented employees, including Yolanda.

Up to that moment in time, Mafalda had no idea that his family was undocumented. Yolanda and Antonio had worked to provide Mafalda and his siblings as normal a life as possible. The family had achieved economic stability; they lived in a middle-class neighborhood; the kids attended good schools; their parents took them to concerts and provided them with other cultural experiences. All at once Yolanda found herself explaining to her children that the reason she had lost her job was that she was undocumented. In fact, she, Antonio, Mafalda, and his twin were all undocumented. And they needed to be careful about how much they disclosed about themselves. To Mafalda, this was a shock. He had never known a life apart from the one they had in the United States. He spoke Spanish because he knew it was important for his parents to retain that part of their cultural heritage, but otherwise he did not feel a strong connection, much less a sense of belonging, to Mexico.

Mafalda's life was suddenly turned upside down. In addition to grappling with this new aspect of his identity, he was now attuned, because of how SB 1070 was circulating in the media, to the virulent anti-immigrant rhetoric that some of his peers at iPoly were espousing. He had just come "out of the closet" in terms of being queer. Now he felt as if he was returning to a different kind of closet because he could not discuss his legal status for fear of social and political backlash. Making matters worse, after years of economic stability Mafalda's parents were now working chaotic hours, and it was apparent that money was tight. The most devastating blow came when Mafalda and his parents approached the counselor at iPoly to discuss Mafalda's participation in the dual enrollment program to earn college credit. Even though Mafalda met the academic requirements to enroll in the program, the counselor refused to enroll him when he learned that Mafalda was undocumented. This led Yolanda and Antonio to take stock of Mafalda's educational situation. They were commuting twenty to thirty minutes each way to take Mafalda to iPoly precisely because they believed that it would provide college options for him. Now they realized that was no longer an option. To Mafalda's dismay, his parents decided to take him out of iPoly and send him to the much closer neighborhood high school.

Mafalda continued to do well in school, but as he approached fall of his senior year, the family realized that it was unlikely they would be able to pay tuition to send him to a four-year public university. Mafalda's dream had been to study biology at the University of California, Santa Barbara. The family had visited the school, and Mafalda was immediately taken by the students riding bicycles across campus; the cool, heavy breeze that reached lecture halls and classrooms; the ocean view from the library. Mafalda and his parents had heard whispers of a new law that California legislators had passed that would grant financial aid to undocumented students, so they were cautiously optimistic when they approached the light-brown-brick student affairs building, where the financial aid office was located. They waited to see a counselor, and when one was available, Mafalda did most of the talking.

He told the counselor that he was undocumented and asked what financial aid might be available to him. The woman fixed Mafalda with a long look, and said, "I'm sorry. There is nothing that we can do for you."

"We've heard there's something called a DREAM Act that provides financial aid for undocumented students," Mafalda answered.

"I don't know what you're talking about with the DREAM Act," the counselor said. "I don't know what that is."

Dazed and frustrated, the family left the office. The sun was now lower in the sky, and the air was quickly turning cold as the family walked to their car. It seemed as if they had reached the end of a road.

Yolanda wanted Mafalda to visit UC Riverside.

"We can't afford it," he said. "I'll go to community college. That's it."

But Yolanda insisted that he at least go to the campus to check it out.

"They're just going to tell us the same thing."

"It's only thirty minutes away. What harm could it do?"

Finally Mafalda agreed.

This time, one of the family's first stops was the financial aid office, and the experience was markedly different. The financial aid counselor explained to Mafalda that there was indeed new legislation that would allow undocumented students to apply for financial aid, but solely through the State of California. (Mafalda would still be ineligible for federal aid.) She said that the policy had been passed but would not go into effect until January 2013. She explained that Mafalda could begin to receive financial aid as soon as the winter quarter of his first year of college.

When she realized that Mafalda would indeed be able to matriculate at a four-year university directly from high school, Yolanda burst into tears. All the years of work advocating for her child's education would matter.[31] It is likely that she did not know Mafalda had been watching her, year after year at his different schools, as she argued with teachers and administrators and pushed for the best possible resources for him. It is likely that Yolanda did not know she was teaching Mafalda about advocacy work.

When Mafalda matriculated at UC Riverside, he was on the lookout for an organization for undocumented students. When he found PODER, he immediately joined, bringing his good humor and willingness to volunteer and desire to advocate for his community—undocumented, Latinx, queer. During his first two years in the group, the two women who were president and vice-president of PODER invited him to attend leadership institutes to sharpen his skills. Mafalda rose to the occasion, and within a couple of years he was the president of PODER. He would welcome new undocumented students to campus and cultivate new leadership among the younger members. When, in the spring of 2015, the UC Office of the President organized its first ever National Summit on Undocumented Students, Mafalda stood on a plush chair in the ballroom of the Oakland Marriott with his fist in the air to protest that the president did not sufficiently include undocumented students in the planning of the event. He subsequently became the Riverside representative of the UC Undocumented Student Coalition, participating in its frequent conference calls to discuss what issues the coalition would put forward at UC Regents meetings.

Undocumented Pedagogies of Home

A few months before the UC Undocumented Student Summit, PODER hosted a public "Coming Out of the Shadows" event. It was a part of a series of events that the group hosted during its annual Immigrant Awareness Week (figure 2.1). Jazmin, Alejandro, and Mafalda all delivered their public testimonios at the event. I was in the crowd of people at the bell tower at the center of campus listening to them talk about what being undocumented meant to them on a public address system that resonated throughout the center of campus. One of the things that struck me was that they all talked about their parents. Mafalda characterized his parents as good people who were willing to do whatever it took to give their child the chance to be healthy. Alejandro reflected on the fear that his parents must have felt when he—their only undocumented son—drove without a license. Jazmin talked about her hardworking her parents and how she was earning her degree for them. I knew then that all of their stories started at home; their *education* about living without papers in this country began with their parents. They arrived at UC Riverside with knowledge that they had gained from their parents about the importance of hard work as well as the exploitation and vulnerability of undocumented labor. Parents had instilled in them an understanding of legal status and their limitations for mobility, the role of police, and possible connections with ICE. However, they had also learned about resilience and advocacy, lessons that would compel them to move

2.1   Display for Immigrant Awareness Week at UC Riverside.
        Courtesy of Daniel Lopez Salas.

forward even when they faced challenges away from home, at the university. The undocumented education that their parents gave them established the foundation of two things: critical consciousness and empowerment. These were key lessons that Jazmin, Alejandro, and Mafalda were able to hone and strengthen in community with one another and the other members of PODER.

3

UNDOCUMENTED LEARNING
AND POLITICAL CONSCIOUSNESS

"Why don't you have a driver's license yet?"

Miguel had heard that question so many times he could almost see the words in bold when he closed his eyes. This time it was a friend who, like him, had enrolled at the local community college after graduating from Arvin High School.

"I don't want a driver's license. I don't need one. Look at me. I'm driving. I don't need one."

"What are you going to do if you get pulled over?"

Growing up, Miguel had spent hours that melted into days on the road with his father, who was a truck driver. Those long drives were some of his best memories as a child; he loved being on the road. To him, driving inspired a sense of freedom and possibility. He was devastated when his parents told him he would not be able to apply for a driver's license; that they would prefer that he limit his driving altogether. Nevertheless, when Miguel graduated from high school, his parents had to give him their reluctant blessing to commute the fifteen miles from their home in one of the small agricultural communities in the Central Valley to community college in Bakersfield every day.

Miguel's drive began on a farm road called Weedpatch Highway. The first six miles of the two-lane road were punctuated by scattered palm trees, almond groves, grape vineyards, an oil refinery, several local trucking companies, and the occasional local market with names such as Mercado Azteca. Once he crossed Highway 58 and into the city limits of Bakersfield, there were some modest homes and strip malls but still the same dustiness; the same hazy views of mountains flanking this southern end of the valley. He always chose to stay on a back road, especially when entering the city limits, to avoid areas where there might be highway patrol. After the road stretched into the brush-covered foothills, he finally merged onto a six-lane highway. He would drive the final five miles of his route toward the exit that would deliver him to the middle-class neighborhood where Bakersfield College was nestled. Sometimes he would spot a security car and suddenly lose his train of thought. He'd feel his shoulders tense up and notice whether his hands were at the ten and two position on the steering wheel. Mostly, however, as Miguel pulled into the school parking lot, his thoughts would gravitate toward his classes for the day, and by the time he was walking toward campus, he felt the same as every other eighteen-year-old student making their way to English 1A or Math 1B.

But Miguel's friend had been with him in high school and knew that he had never gone to the department of motor vehicles for his test. He hadn't gone not because he thought he wouldn't pass the test. He had thrived academically in high school—all advanced placement and honors classes, extracurricular activities. Most of his close friends had gone away to University of California (UC) schools.[1] This friend knew that Miguel had been accepted to several colleges and universities, too, but had chosen community college to save money. Miguel knew that his friend wanted to know what was holding him back, but he didn't want to tell her. Rather, he simply replied, "I'm a good driver," hoping that she might think that he was being anti-authority by driving without a license. On another day with another friend he might compare his driving record with theirs. "Who's been pulled over more—me or you?" In each of these conversations, he tried to keep it light and to change the subject as soon as possible.

The truth was that Miguel did want a driver's license, but he was not eligible for one, just as he had been ineligible for the financial aid that would have helped him to enroll in one of the four-year colleges that had granted him admission. He had migrated to the United States as a toddler and had never felt different from his friends or classmates. It was only in his last two years of high school that Miguel realized that, without a Social Security number, his life would be different from theirs.

The only people who knew about his situation apart from his family were school staff. In high school, his beloved Ms. Morales, the teacher who ran the career resource center, investigated how he would navigate admissions and financial aid as an undocumented student. She was the one who told him, "Tell the financial aid counselors that you're an AB 540 student. They'll know what to do."[2] When he went to enroll, the financial aid counselors had him fill out a California Nonresident Exemption request form, on which he had to indicate that he had attended high school in California, had graduated, and would adjust his immigration status given the opportunity. With the submission of this form, Miguel would qualify for in-state tuition. The financial aid counselors referred to him as an "AB 540 student," which seemed to him to be a euphemism for what some might call "illegal" or what many in his community might refer to as "sin papeles" (without papers). Beyond the financial aid office, he wouldn't tell anyone else.

Miguel never thought that he might meet other students in his same situation, let alone build a community. Given the region's dependence on undocumented farm labor and the fact that the financial aid office counselors knew how to process his AB 540 paperwork, he knew that there were other students at school in his same situation. But he carried the shame of being different from his friends; he didn't want to expose himself by openly looking for other people like him. Furthermore, his parents had warned him not to let anyone know. "If you expose yourself, you expose all of us." He thought about what his parents had sacrificed for him and his sister to have a life in the United States. They regularly recounted to their children how they had crossed the border through the desert in conditions so harrowing they were unsure they would survive. Miguel would honor their sacrifice by keeping their family secret and focusing on school.

Since he was completing his general education at Bakersfield College, Miguel thought he might be able to afford two years at a UC campus. The messages he got in his honors classes were that UC schools were the best in the state because their professors had research agendas and could provide a more cutting-edge education. When his friends returned home for holidays, he jealously listened to their stories of school and did whatever work he could to ensure that he would be able to attend a UC school as a transfer student. He searched websites for information about transferring and realized that as long as he completed the courses listed on a form called the Intersegmental General Education Transfer Curriculum (IGETC), he would be able to matriculate at one of the UC campuses.[3] After two years of commuting to community college and steadily checking off the courses on the IGETC, he was poised to transfer to UC Riverside.

Education and Critical Consciousness

When we think of how education occurs in the US public school system, we first think about how students learn academic subjects in their classrooms. Less frequently we might imagine how schools' academic and social contexts shape how young people learn about society and their place in it. In this chapter, I emphasize undocumented education that happens in college but outside the doors of its classrooms and lecture halls. This education occurs in conversations among students; during exchanges in university administration offices; and especially in student organizations, among other places on campus. I argue that these informal sites of education outside the classroom can powerfully shape the identities, critical consciousness, and political awakening of unauthorized youth, especially because their undocumented legal status forces some level of political awareness. While most undocumented young people become aware of their legal status in high school, it is not so much an *identity* as it is a *status* that curtails opportunities and poses new challenges. For some of these students, the experience of college becomes more than an opportunity for a career that promotes economic stability. It includes political education both in and outside the classroom, as well as the creation of politicized identities. Developing politicized, undocumented identities leads students to claim rights, to further educate themselves about rights and resources that are available to them, and, most important, to educate and advocate for their communities.

Most undocumented students are not political radicals. As a group, these young people are similar to other first-generation students who attend college with the goal of greater financial stability for themselves and their families. However, when considering the broad spectrum of civic engagement, undocumented students are more involved in their communities than their citizen counterparts.[4] Their civic engagement might include joining an organization to help solve a community problem, talking to people about political issues, or outright public protest.[5] Civic and political involvement has the potential to educate young people about community issues, raise political consciousness, cultivate political community, and build a skill set to organize around political issues.

This chapter examines how undocumented forms of education within college and university contexts shape the identities and political consciousness of the young people who became involved in Providing Opportunities, Dreams, and Education in Riverside (PODER) between 2010 and 2014. I approach this analysis by drawing primarily from Leisy Ábrego's insightful "Legal Consciousness of Undocumented Latinos," in which she outlines the differences in identity and political consciousness between first generation migrants and their 1.5-generation children.[6] Ábrego's argument is based on segmented assimilation theory: the idea that immigrants experience and are incorporated into the United States differently based on the segment of society to which they assimilate. She asserts that adult migrants often feel the weight of their undocumented legal status immediately because they incorporate into mainstream US society through the labor market, where they face limited employment options, an inability to file grievances without fear of repercussions, and, of course, anxiety about Immigration and Customs Enforcement (ICE) raids at their places of work. Those who migrate as children, by contrast, incorporate themselves into US life and culture largely through the public school system, where they are instructed to speak English and learn about US history and are acculturated with a cohort that includes American-born peers.[7] Because of this early education, undocumented young people do not readily distinguish themselves from their peers. When they realize that they have a different legal status (usually in high school), they understand for the first time how their legal status makes them distinct from their US-born peers. This is so, at least in part, because legal status dovetails with social status, as undocumented students grapple with being unable to mark the same milestones as their friends (e.g., obtaining a driver's license, registering to vote). While these youths have learned to be "American" (or, at least, American Latinx), their legal status is at odds with their social identity, which leads them to feel isolation, stigma, or shame.[8] This is not to say that undocumented adults do not feel stigmatized or that undocumented youth do not feel anxiety. Certainly, both immigrant generations grapple with those feelings at different moments.[9] In fact, undocumented young people fear for the safety of family members who are more easily targeted by ICE during workplace raids.[10] I use Ábrego's framework in this chapter to help elucidate how the persistence of stigma and fear affect how undocumented youth develop their political identities.[11]

Ábrego reminds us, however, that legal consciousness is not stagnant; the ethnography in this chapter highlights how students develop politicized legal consciousness in college. College students are almost stereotypically politically engaged, but there are reasons that the university experience lends itself to the development of political consciousness and activism. Students have the opportunity to take courses about US and global politics, learning and critiquing flows of power; they meet peers from outside their home communities who often have divergent political viewpoints, which might broaden their own political purviews; and they have the ability to join organizations that engage with social and political issues. This political education frames the experiences of most college students, but the depth of their involvement varies. For those students whose daily lives are directly affected by public policy, such political contexts can provide the spark that ignites a critical, political consciousness. The Brazilian educator Paulo Freire's concept of critical pedagogy illuminates such shifts in consciousness as a direct result of education—the kind of education that teaches people to read both "the word" and "the world."[12] For these students, the education that they receive in college—both in and outside of the classroom—can powerfully shape their legal consciousness and political identities.

Not so common in our understanding of the political education that college students receive is the effect of community building and student organizations. The transition to a college/university opens possibilities for students to see themselves (and the world in which they live) in different ways. The education scholar Tara Yosso argues that Chicano/a students experience three stages of adjustment as they move into spaces of higher education: culture shock, community building, and critical navigation among multiple worlds.[13] For the undocumented students in my study, connecting to student organizations that provided a safe space to talk about their unique experiences and to know that they were not alone was a social and emotional lifeline.[14] Such organizations provide the possibility of leadership training, as well as opportunities to engage in community service both on and off campus. Though the students in my study did not necessarily identify as "Chicano/a/x," community building in such spaces, especially with other undocumented students and allies, was a key stage in their political development because it helped to mitigate the feelings of isolation, shame, and stigma that emerged in high school. Destigmatizing their legal status and mobilizing politicized identities in its place allows undocumented young people to challenge perceptions of immigrants and immigration laws and to advocate for increased educational access for other undocumented youth.

While I have emphasized work and school as the primary contexts that shape the political identities of first- and 1.5-generation undocumented immigrants, the larger political context and attitudes toward immigrants is also significant. This research includes the perspectives of students who entered college during a period in which immigration policy was rapidly changing. Despite the repeated failure of the US Congress to pass a Development, Relief, and Education for Alien Minors (DREAM) Act, which would have granted a pathway to citizenship for undocumented young people, the passage of Deferred Action for Childhood Arrivals (DACA) in 2012 and key California state legislation passed between 2011 and 2013 created a more hospitable state environment for the undocumented community, especially its youth. The California DREAM Act (2011) rendered undocumented young people eligible for state financial aid to attend college, and those eligible for DACA (2012) were granted a two-year reprieve from deportation and temporary work permits. Finally, California's State Assembly Bill (AB) 60 (2013) allowed undocumented Californians to apply for driver's licenses. There were different stakes for undocumented youth who entered college before 2011 compared with those who entered afterward. There was more stigma and more fear of repercussions for those undocumented students who were "out" prior to DACA, in addition to far less available financial support. As a professor from 2006 through this period of legislative change, I noticed a difference in how PODER—as a group—presented itself to the campus community. However, there were always students who were more open about their status, regardless of the time period. This chapter explores two students' stories and their paths toward politicization.

Finally, this research accounts for undocumented students who are politically active, which indicates highly developed political consciousness. Even among politicized youth, however, shame, stigma, and fear persist. As students chant "Undocumented! Unafraid!" at protests and rallies, they might still feel the undercurrent of those negative emotions. But the affirmation of their marginalized identities and the boldness of their public proclamations—especially in community with others—help to keep those feelings at bay. Though these assertive young people are a minority among undocumented students on campus, they can teach us invaluable lessons about how education occurs outside the classroom and how it can have deep community and social impact.

Becoming Undocumented

At his transfer orientation during the spring of 2010, Miguel met another incoming Latino student, Henry, and the two of them got along well. This was a relief to Miguel because he had arrived at UC Riverside knowing no one else. When classes started, they planned to meet for lunch at the Highlander Union Building (HUB), a type of student union on campus. It was a Wednesday, and they soon realized that on Wednesdays the campus hosted "nooners"—midday events at which dozens of student organizations set up tables around the bell tower at the center of campus to recruit new members. Music by a live band playing nondescript rock music was blaring as hundreds of students passed through on their way from classes to the HUB. Henry told Miguel, "Hey, dude, I'm thinking about joining UER [La Unión Estudiantil de la Raza]. Do you want to go check out their table?"

Though Miguel had been involved in student organizations in high school, his involvement in extracurriculars had waned at his community college, and he did not have a strong opinion yet about any student organizations at UC Riverside. Still, Henry was his only friend, so he agreed to go with him to the UER table.

UER appealed to Miguel right away. It was like a fraternity, but with a focus on the Latino community. After that day at the bell tower, Miguel and Henry went to meetings to learn more about the group. Miguel started to get to know some current UER members, as well as the other guys who were "rushing" alongside him. Most were Latino, though there were a few brothers who were Black and Asian. A lot of them interspersed Spanish words and phrases with their English, as people did back home, and he realized that several came from small agricultural communities very similar to his hometown. Moving to Southern California—a place that he associated with urban sprawl—Miguel never considered that he might meet other students from farmworker families. The UER space felt different from the larger campus.[15] For Miguel, it felt like a home away from home.

As Miguel and his cohort of twelve prepared to formally enter the group, UER leadership dedicated one meeting to a "unity building" exercise. Each week UER meetings were held in a classroom or some other, similar space on campus. That night, the group was meeting in Watkins Hall, where Miguel would later take many of the political science classes required for his major. The fluorescent light in the room made the white floor tiles gleam as the guys filed in and began to rearrange the desks into a circle, making small talk about their classes—which were going to be a lot of work and had gotten off to a good start. The leader of the group's meeting that night let them all settle into their seats before beginning the evening's activity.

"Now that we are going to become brothers," he began, "tonight we're going to share something about ourselves that we would only share among family. I'm going to give you some time to think. What is something about you that only your family knows? We're going to go around the circle and share with each other."

As Miguel began to reflect on this question, the first thing that came to mind was his family's secret about being undocumented. Over the past few weeks, getting to know the members of UER, Miguel had felt a sense of brotherhood, of family. This was a secret he felt he could entrust to them. In those few minutes, he decided that he would tell them about his status.

He fidgeted in his seat as the first couple of guys took their turns sharing. He felt his chest tightening as he looked around the circle to gauge the reactions to what his soon-to-be brothers were saying. He became aware of his breath.

Then it was his turn.

"I don't have a Social Security number."

He could hear himself talking, but at the same time he could almost see himself and the other members of the group looking at him.

"My parents brought me here when I was little, and we don't have papers."

The tightness in his chest was rising into this throat.

"I can't get a driver's license, and I don't qualify for financial aid."

As his eyes began to sting, Miguel blinked rapidly, knowing that he needed to finish.

"I've never told anybody. The only people who know are my family."

He exhaled and looked for a reaction from the UER brother who was facilitating.

"Thank you for sharing," he said.

The brother next to Miguel put his hand on his shoulder. "Bro, it's OK. I have family like that, too. Don't even worry about it."

More murmurs of support followed.

"Don't worry. Your secret is safe with us."

"Don't even worry about it."

The facilitator moved on to the next person before Miguel could fully understand what had just happened. He had disclosed his status out loud in front of a group of people whom he had met just a couple of months earlier. And they had been supportive. They understood. They had family like him.

Miguel wasn't able to focus on anyone else's personal stories after he had spoken. His family back home had guarded this secret so closely. He thought that revealing it would be more dramatic. He thought he would be judged or looked down on when the other members of the group realized that he was different from them; he had braced himself for rejection. What he experienced that night, however, was acceptance and sympathy. Coming out at that UER meeting pierced the isolation and shame that he had felt as a teenager in the Central Valley. It was not just that he had a new group of friends; it was that these friends were familiar with his situation. For the rest of that school year Miguel continued to be discreet about his undocumented status, but UER changed something for him: it provided a space where he felt accepted and part of a community.

Miguel's experience with UER underscores the importance of safe spaces for undocumented students on college campuses. Scholars have argued that such safe spaces are critical for students who historically have been excluded or marginalized in institutions of higher education because they provide a sense of belonging.[16] Yosso argues that the kind of community building that occurs in these spaces helps students transition to college and begin to develop a consciousness to critically navigate their home communities and the university.[17] For Miguel, UER provided the space to move past his feelings of shame and stigma to finally reveal his undocumented status to his peers, and that revelation gave him a critical awareness that he was not alone. He had a community on campus with whom he could let his guard down and reveal the parts of himself that he had previously kept hidden. This was the first step in thinking about being undocumented not just as a status, but as an identity—one of which he did not necessarily have to be ashamed. And, I suggest, it was a first step toward developing a political consciousness.

Just a few miles away, at Riverside City College (RCC), another undocumented young person was also coming to terms with her status in an academic safe space: an English classroom affiliated with the Puente Project.

Reading the World through Puente

Most of the other students Italia knew who were also beginning at RCC were enrolled in English 1A.[18] It was one of the general education classes that she would need to transfer to a four-year university. Though she did not speak English when she arrived in the United States as a ten year old, Italia had learned the language quickly. She would always remember that her fifth-grade teacher had tried to involve her in the classroom conversations even though Italia did not yet understand the language. The teacher had another student translate for her, and she labeled some basic items in the classroom for Italia—door, window, bathroom. These words slowly became a vocabulary that she could use to communicate with her teacher and her peers. By the time she was in junior high, she was placed in mainstream English classes, and in high school she read canonical works in English such as the Gettysburg Address and plays by Shakespeare and Arthur Miller. She crafted thesis statements and tried to support her arguments with quotes from the texts. Italia imagined that English 1A would be the college version of the college prep English classes she had taken in high school. She knew, however, that there would be at least one difference. At RCC, she would be in the English 1A class affiliated with its Puente Project.

Puente was established in Northern California in 1981 to help address the low levels of Latinx students who completed four-year college degrees by focusing on writing, counseling, and mentorship.[19] Italia did not feel as if she would need extra academic support, but a friend who had graduated from her high school a year earlier explained that Puente courses would replace her required English courses and give her priority enrollment for other classes. Having heard that many of the core classes needed to transfer were impacted and sometimes difficult to enroll in, Italia decided to submit an application to join Puente, and she was accepted.

Italia walked into the Arthur G. Paul Quadrangle, the oldest building on the RCC campus, where most of the English classes were housed. Riverside City College had not been her first choice. She had wanted to go straight to a four-year college or university from high school, but her family could not afford the expense. She had been fighting the feeling that RCC would be like an extension of high school, knowing that many of her high school classmates would also be attending this community college. Walking into this building, however, made her feel like she was in college. The hundred-year-old stone arches that lead into the building and an open space in the middle of the quadrangle felt collegiate. Through the pillars of the main walkways, she could see her peers making their way to class or sitting and reading on benches perched on grass that seemed impossibly green in the bright morning sun. She walked around the quad scanning the numbers on the doors until she located her classroom. Opening the door, Italia regarded its tile floors and individual desks facing a larger teacher's desk and a whiteboard. She took a seat toward the middle of the room and waited while the other students filled their seats and the teacher, Steven Garcia, distributed the course syllabus.

Italia could see by the syllabus that this course, unlike English courses that she had previously taken, included writing by several authors with Spanish surnames, and the content of the fiction and nonfiction that they would be reviewing that semester would primarily be about the US Latinx community. The assignments would be similar to ones that she had completed before—first drafts and final drafts of essays—but Mr. Garcia seemed to have expectations beyond grammatically correct writing or even the "correct" analysis. He impressed on the students that he wasn't looking for rote answers. Rather, he wanted to hear their perspectives; he wanted them to bring what they knew into classroom discussions, assignments, and, especially, the arguments in their papers. This unnerved Italia slightly as she was unsure which parts of what she knew would be academically relevant. She was eighteen and saw herself as a normal teenager. What could she offer that was different?

Over the next several weeks, Italia read and wrote as she would have in any English class. In this class, however, she found herself reading historical narratives and nonfiction essays in addition to literature, and all of it was outside of the canon of works she had learned in high school. Of everything that Italia was reading, the histories affected her the most. She had loved her US history classes in high school. Even though she was Mexican by birth, she was enthralled by stories of US independence, westward expansion, and the Civil Rights Movement. She never noticed the absence of Mexican people from those narratives. Most of the people of Mexican origin she knew had immigrated over the previous twenty years; she didn't imagine that her community had much to do with the longer arc of US history. Then she read about the Chicano/a Movement of the 1960s and 1970s. She didn't consider herself a Chicana (Chicana seemed to refer to Mexican Americans who had been in the United States for a long time), but she was drawn to these Mexican American chapters of US history. She started to piece together what she knew about the US Southwest having been part of Mexico before the Mexican-American War with subsequent waves of immigration and labor struggles throughout the twentieth century. She started to question why she had never learned these particular histories before.

Though this version of US history was unfamiliar to Italia, several of her peers in class had already learned it. Some of them had strong opinions about why their history had been excluded from mainstream US history and offered additional information and perspectives from what they had learned in their high school Movimiento Estudiantil Chicano de Aztlán (MEChA) clubs.[20] While Mr. Garcia would nod and ask these students questions to deepen their analysis during class discussion, Italia listened almost jealously, feeling as if she had missed out on a critical piece of education. She was eager to catch up, reading voraciously and working to crystallize her thoughts and arguments in her written assignments. Through this process, she began to feel as if a window was being opened for her. It wasn't just about getting the good grades that would allow her to transfer to a competitive four-year college or university; it was about developing an academic identity. She was beginning to see things from a critical perspective; she was beginning to understand the interconnectedness of historical and contemporary narratives, and she could see that she—even as a relatively recent immigrant—was part of that narrative arc.[21]

In addition to the English sequence, the Puente Project required students to participate in the Puente Club. It met in classrooms on campus after hours or sometimes in one of the brightly lit rooms in the library. A major focus of the club was to expose its students to what life would be like after they transferred from community college to a four-year college or university. The group organized fundraising events to pay for campus tours to colleges and universities throughout California. While the Puente program's primary focus was on increasing the number of Latinx students who received bachelor's degrees, an additional goal set by Mr. Garcia and other Puente teachers at RCC was for students to develop a civic identity, which Italia understood as being involved in her community. The Puente Club had subcommittees that provided space for students to talk about different social and political issues that affected the Latinx community and for students to discuss how to address them. One of those was the AB 540 subcommittee.

The label "AB 540" was a new one for Italia. When she had left Mexico City at age ten with her mother and brother, she was old enough to understand that they were migrating without papers. It was the year 2000, and her father had been working in the United States over the previous year. In that time, he had been able to save enough money for his wife and two children to cross, as well.[22] He believed that Italia and her brother would have better lives in the United States. Living without papers was a family sacrifice. Italia accepted that she wouldn't be able to do all the same things that her peers could do. She and her family could not return to Mexico to visit her grandparents. She wasn't able to get a driver's license. She didn't register to vote. She didn't qualify for financial aid for college. The last one stung more than the rest as she watched several of her friends make plans to leave home for college. Up to that moment, not having papers was just a matter of fact. Italia's parents didn't make her feel as if she needed to hide her status; they never made her feel as if she should be afraid or embarrassed. Some migrants had papers, and some did not. It was only when she was preparing to apply to colleges along with her friends that Italia first felt the weight of being undocumented. In the Puente Club—and, more specifically, in the AB 540 subcommittee—she realized that she was not alone.

When Mr. Garcia and the other Puente staff talked about civic engagement, Italia had initially understood it in the broadest of terms: being involved in her community. Within the AB 540 subcommittee, however, Italia saw that civic engagement could be focused, and it could make a direct and sometimes immediate impact. Members of the AB 540 subcommittee decided that they wanted to help other undocumented students navigate the bureaucracy and the expense of college. To achieve the latter goal, they organized fundraisers that were separate from the general Puente Club. The events were intended to help students such as Italia—who did not qualify for financial aid—to stay afloat. Even though AB 540 legislation made it possible for Italia to pay the same rate of tuition as everyone else, college was expensive. She had to pay for textbooks, school supplies, printing, a bus pass. Italia had a job to help with the expenses, but the Puente / AB 540 scholarship fundraisers were critical to her ability to stay in school. Italia began to help coordinate outreach efforts with the group so that other undocumented students could learn about the resources that the Puente AB 540 subcommittee was generating, as well as any other resources they discovered that were accessible to undocumented students. Moreover, working together with her fellow Puentistas and just *being* together made the stress of college more manageable.

Through conversations with other students, faculty, and staff, Italia and her peers learned that if they formalized themselves as a club independent of Puente, their organization would be eligible for additional funding through the college. Italia could see that she and her undocumented peers in Puente were walking a fine line with the college administration. Trusted professors advised Italia and her peers not to refer to the group as an "undocumented" club but to think about language that would not seem "political" or partisan to the administration. This gave Italia pause. Even though she had been raised to understand her status as a matter of fact, she was beginning to see that even the way that people—her peers, her professors, and the college administration— talked about legal status provoked strong reactions. Ultimately, the group decided to call itself Students Advocating for Education (SAFE). Italia and her peers wanted to broaden access to higher education as a primary goal, but they also wanted other undocumented students on campus to know that they would have a safe space in the group. Italia was excited when the group received notice from the university that they were an officially recognized student organization. She knew that they had just opened a possibility to make life better for other undocumented students at RCC.

Italia's experience in Puente was a critical moment along her path toward developing a political consciousness. For her, political consciousness began with deepening her academic identity. Reading literary and historical perspectives from Mexican Americans in the United States opened the space for Italia to critically engage the world around her. This type of education—in this case, an ethnic studies curriculum—was akin to what Freire refers to as "problem-posing" education that helps students "develop their power to perceive critically *the way they exist* in the world *with which* and *in which* they find themselves."[23] Freire argues that this education helps students to see the world not as a static reality, but as a reality that can be transformed.[24] This was the case for Italia. Especially because her Puente classroom education occurred in tandem with civic engagement, she felt empowered not only to question the status quo, but to change it. These lessons were made even more powerful because they occurred in community with other Latinx and undocumented students. Like Miguel, who began to feel his experience normalized and accepted in the context of UER, Italia felt that she was and could be part of something bigger and, significantly, that she could effect social change.

Joining PODER

It didn't occur to Miguel the night of the UER talking circle that there might be another undocumented person in the room. Victor was also a transfer student, but from the Riverside area, and he was part of the cohort that was rushing UER that fall. Even though he was reserved, Victor always came across as confident and sociable. Miguel knew that he was a premed student who was involved not only with UER but also with other student organizations. After a year of getting to know him through UER meetings, service events, and socials, Miguel had no idea that Victor was also undocumented. Then, at the beginning of their second year as transfer students, Victor sent a text message to Miguel: "What do you think about joining PODER?"

Miguel had attended a few PODER meetings when he first arrived at UC Riverside at the recommendation of the director of the Office of Chicano

Student Programs. He had disclosed his legal status to her to see whether she knew of any scholarships for which he could apply. She directed him to PODER without giving him much information about the group. Even after attending some meetings, Miguel did not fully understand the purpose of the organization. He knew it had something to do with education and that it held a scholarship banquet at the end of every school year. Otherwise, it was unclear to him what the group did or what its purpose was. He found members of the group to be friendly but guarded, almost as if they didn't trust him. After attending a few meetings, Miguel decided not to return. He remembered that Victor had also attended some of those PODER meetings, and he had apparently continued to do so throughout the winter and spring. By the end of that school year, Victor had been elected president of PODER.

There had been some tension between members of PODER who wanted the group to engage in advocacy work for immigrant communities and those who wanted it to be a support group for undocumented students. Because most of the leadership of the group was graduating, Victor saw the opportunity to create something new. He knew that many students felt vulnerable revealing their status; not many would be likely to approach the organization's table at a nooner and risk being identified as undocumented. Even current members of the group hesitated to volunteer to sit at the PODER table to recruit members for fear of revealing their status. To build the group's membership, Victor decided to reach out personally to friends and other people he knew who were either undocumented or likely to be allies.

When PODER resumed in the fall of 2011 it had about ten members, but because of work schedules, only six or seven regularly attended the weekly meetings. Victor would prepare an agenda, but he always prioritized people's check-ins. Sometimes students would arrive at the meetings crying from the stress or frustration of not being able to pay their tuition or not being able to pay their rent; from getting pulled over and being caught driving without a license or their car being towed; from anxiety about an immigration raid or the deportation of a family member. In his mind, PODER should first and foremost be a safe space for students to share the parts of their lives that they might not feel comfortable disclosing elsewhere. While everyone in the group showed sympathy and support, each person chose how much they wanted to reveal about themselves.[25]

This was the PODER that Miguel joined at the beginning of his second year at UC Riverside. It was in those conversations with other PODER members that Miguel began to understand what connected the members of the group, and he began to feel connected, too. He intimately understood financial struggle. Though he worked in the agricultural fields of the Central Valley during summers and saved money for college, he was facing substantially more expenses at UC Riverside than he had when he was living at home and commuting to the local community college. Not only were tuition and fees significantly higher, but some of his textbooks cost in the hundreds of dollars and he now had the added expenses of rent and food. Like him, many of the other members of PODER spent a considerable amount of time researching scholarships and completing applications. Because they knew that every hundred dollars made a difference, they shared scholarship information with one another. Moreover, they organized and hosted a scholarship banquet for undocumented UC Riverside students during the spring of each year.[26]

Miguel also realized that many of the other members of PODER had the same challenges he had with UC Riverside's financial aid counselors. Even though AB 540 had been a policy for a decade, many financial aid counselors were still unfamiliar with it. Miguel and other PODER members had to explain the financial aid policy to UC Riverside employees, downloading information from government sources and presenting it to them along with their already filled-out paperwork.[27] Taking the time to research and apply for scholarships and taking the time to educate financial aid counselors about state policy was a significant commitment. The hours Miguel spent in these endeavors were almost like taking an additional course—one that he needed to take to keep himself financially afloat. It was gratifying for him to know that he was not the only person who had these experiences with financial aid; these were students to whom he could deeply relate. He was grateful to realize that he wasn't alone. There were other students on campus who intimately understood the experience of being an undocumented undergraduate student. They were in it together.

Miguel started to attend PODER meetings regularly and became more involved. He recruited other people to the group because he knew the power of those conversations, the ability to discuss in a safe space the things many of them held in secret. Through this process, Miguel was becoming more self-assured, more comfortable in his own skin. He and his fellow PODER members understood that their small community of undocumented students at UC Riverside extended beyond the campus. The group held a conference for high school students each fall to educate the students and their parents about the policies and the scholarship information that would make it easier for them to attend college. These were policies that PODER had researched; financial aid strategies that the group had come up with.

The group held panels during these conferences when undocumented students would speak about their experiences navigating UC Riverside as undocumented people. Miguel began to selectively disclose his status to other people—primarily undocumented high school students and their parents. It wasn't so long ago that he was like those students, unsure of whether it would be possible to transfer to a four-year university; unclear about the bureaucracy of the university; anxious about how he and his family would make financial ends meet. Coming out as undocumented to these students was important because they might be able to see themselves in him. He was undocumented, and he was making his way. Miguel was never fully comfortable with public speaking and even less so disclosing his legal status, but he understood that saying it aloud had a powerful impact on people. It began to have an impact on him, as well.

Just like Italia, Miguel had started calling himself an AB 540 student during community college, and like her, he recognized that identifying as AB 540 rather than "undocumented" made people outside his community more comfortable. Frankly, it made him feel more comfortable. However, sharing his story in these undocumented spaces—these informal spaces of education on and off campus—Miguel could feel himself shedding the stigma of that word, healing from the years of shame that accompanied it. "Undocumented" was not just a status; it was a political identity. When he referred to himself as undocumented, he understood that he belonged to a community of people who had similar experiences of navigating their "illegality" at school and in the public sphere. Furthermore, this community of undocumented people were also deeply invested in creating pathways to college for other young people without papers. Miguel was completing his degree in philosophy, law, and society, with the goal of attending law school and becoming an immigration attorney so he could help families like his own. The work PODER was doing with younger generations of students dovetailed with this goal. He started to think: *I can definitely do this. We need to do this.* His undocumented identity was not just politicized; it also held a specific political mission to serve the migrant community.

SAFE and the California Dream Network

Just as the Puente Club had created a subcommittee for undocumented student issues, the Los Angeles–based Coalition for Humane Immigrant Rights (CHIRLA) created a suborganization called the California Dream Network (CDN) to support undocumented young people and build leadership within their ranks.[28] During its inception in the early 2000s, the CDN did outreach to student organizations on college campuses that were working to address the needs of undocumented students. The CDN identified SAFE at RCC and invited student representatives from the group to attend a three-day retreat at California State University, Fresno, where they could learn more about immigration-related political issues and how to build their leadership skills.

It was January 2009, and Italia and four other members of the newly formed undocumented student organization SAFE decided to make the trip to Fresno. She did not know much about CHIRLA or the CDN, but she was excited about what she would learn. It would not be Italia's first time out of Southern California (when she was growing up her family had taken vacations driving to Northern California), but it would her first time traveling alone with her peers. One of her friends had a car that seated five, so they decided that he would drive, and they would take turns sitting in the front and back seats. As they left the Inland Empire and began to drive west, Italia noted the familiar tangle of Los Angeles freeways and, finally, the I-5 north over the base of the hulking Sierra Nevada mountains, a steep pass known simply as the Grapevine. As they descended the mountains, Italia could see the entire Central Valley laid out before them without a large city in sight, just miles and miles of fields. She could distinguish citrus groves and grape vineyards but mostly did not know what crops were growing. Before long, they merged on to Highway 99, which she knew would take them to Fresno. Along this stretch she saw occasional packing sheds and oil-derrick pumps, moving up and down like giant sculptural birds pecking the earth for worms. After about an hour they finally entered the Bakersfield city limits and knew it wouldn't be long before they were in Fresno. They continued north through Delano, which, she remembered from what she had read in Puente, was where Mexican and Filipino farmworkers launched the United Farm Workers union and the grape boycott during the 1960s and 1970s.[29] While this history had loomed large for Italia, they drove through the town in just a few minutes, noting only a couple of fast food restaurants, gas stations, and hotels along the highway.

Italia was anxious to get out of the car by the time they arrived in Fresno and made another freeway change, now moving toward the northwestern part of the city, where the campus was located. As her friends navigated with the directions the CDN sent, Italia realized that Cal State Fresno was the biggest college campus she had ever seen. The buildings were boxy, straight lines with flat roofs and in muted tones; they were not usually more than a couple of stories tall, but they were large, and the campus was sprawling. Grateful to park and finally stretch her legs, Italia walked with her friends to the student union, where they found other students registering for the CDN retreat. The people who were working the registration tables also seemed to be students, all about their age and casually dressed. Italia reviewed the folder she was given at registration, which contained the agenda for the weekend, a map of the campus, and information about where she and her friends from SAFE would be staying.

They would be spending the two nights of the event with undergraduate students from Cal State Fresno who were also active in an undocumented student organization. Soon after they arrived, Italia found herself piling back into the car to drive the short distance from campus to the students' apartment complex. The apartments were modest, and it seemed as if there were more college students than families living in them. Italia wondered what it must be like to be this kind of college student, living apart from her family and with friends and surrounded by other young people. That first night, she and her friends spent hours talking with the students from Fresno, who were curious about what life was like in Southern California, so close to Los Angeles, and lamented that there was not much to do in Fresno. Italia and her friends had questions about CDN and how they would be spending the next two days. Italia felt a connection with the Fresno students because, like her, they knew what it was like to be a college student without papers. She was also growing excited about the other people she would meet at the retreat and the conversations they would have.

The next morning Italia noticed more students arriving at the campus. As far as she could tell, they were all Latinx, most speaking in English, some in Spanish, some moving back and forth between the two languages. She could see from their name tags that they came from different parts of the state. Some were from community colleges like her, and others were from four-year universities, including some UC campuses. These made the biggest impression on her. She thought, *Wow, these kids, they're undocumented, they don't have any financial assistance and they're doing it.* She could feel a palpable energy as they all began to file into a large room in the student union for the first session of the day. The speaker who was leading the session was Maria Rodriguez, the statewide organizer for the California Dream Network.[30] There were about fifty students in the room, and as they all took their seats, Maria welcomed them to Fresno and to the retreat. She was a petite woman with curly hair and a broad smile who barely looked older than they did. As she began to speak, Italia realized that Maria had been organizing around immigration, and especially educational access for undocumented young people, over the past decade. As a high school student, she had been part of the successful campaign to pass AB 540; there were rumors that there was a picture of her flanking Governor Gray Davis when he signed the bill into law.

That day Maria conveyed both energy and optimism about the moment of possibility that they were in. Barack Obama had just been elected president and would soon be inaugurated. After eight years of a presidential administration that had overseen dramatic immigration restrictions and surveillance after September 11 and the construction of six hundred miles of a border wall along the US-Mexico border, Maria and her fellow organizers at CHIRLA were optimistic about the possibility of immigration reform.[31] She gave them an overview of the day: how they would be deepening their knowledge about local, state, and federal immigration regulations and potential policies, as well as develop their leadership skills. She warned them that it would be an intense day, but that she and the other organizers had built in time for them to reflect and to ground themselves. "We are doing important work for our communities, but," she impressed on them, "we also have to be accountable for our own self-preservation." With that idea echoing in her mind, Italia headed among the crowd to her first breakout session.

She had to choose between "Intro to Organizing," where she might learn concrete political strategies, and "Story of Self," where she could refine how she told her immigration story in a way that might motivate lawmakers to see the human impact of immigration policy. For students who were at more advanced stages of their political development, there were sessions such as "How to Create a Dream Resource Center on Your Campus" and "How to Mount a Know Your Rights Campaign."[32] Regardless of what students chose, afterward everyone would meet as a large group to report back. As Maria had promised, Italia had time between meetings to wander around the campus—sometimes by herself and sometimes with other young people from the retreat—to reflect on what she was learning and to talk through some of the new ideas presented to her. At the same time that her experience that weekend was deepening her relationships with her peers from SAFE, she was also making important connections with undocumented students across the state. These would be relationships that she would draw on for support for years to come.

At the end of the day, the group came together to decide which policies the CDN should prioritize over the next year. It seemed to Italia that there were two camps. The first was advocating for a piecemeal approach that would advocate for federal legislation such as the DREAM Act, which would help only a small cross-section of the undocumented community: young people who had been brought to the United States by their parents.[33] Italia understood that she would benefit from a policy such as this. However, several students wanted comprehensive immigration reform, which would benefit their families and communities. The problem was that the latter option had been met with tremendous resistance from Republican lawmakers, whereas the DREAM Act had some Republican support. People made the argument that it would be more feasible to pass piecemeal legislation, starting with young people and then advocating for the broader undocumented community. Italia thought it made sense to focus on so-called Dreamers such as herself, but she also understood the pain of leaving her parents behind in this process. She thought especially about her father, who was relentlessly optimistic. "Lo principal es pensar que algo bueno viene" (It's important to think something good is coming), he would say to her. He had started a business as a taquero with very few resources. He never complained about the difficulties; he just kept pushing forward. If there was anyone who *deserved* citizenship, it was him. Italia heard the emotional arguments that her peers were making about these issues, and she felt them in her gut. She mostly listened and observed the debates, thinking about her parents and the families of all the young people in that room, and quietly wiped tears from her face.[34]

After the emotionally charged closing session, Italia was grateful that Maria had opened space for the students to recenter themselves. Maria acknowledged for Italia and the other participants that their feelings were valid. For them, immigration was personal, and there was no shame in feeling angry, scared, betrayed, sad, or any combination of those emotions. Though Italia was still processing her emotions, she felt affirmed when Maria acknowledged that their political development was not just cerebral; it was something that they felt in their bodies. Maria led the group through grounding exercises. She instructed them to close their eyes to focus on their breathing; to plant their feet on the floor and feel the ground beneath them. With her eyes closed Italia heard Maria's soothing voice telling them to breathe, to focus on exhaling the negative emotions. Italia could feel her heart rate slow and some of the tension leaving her body. When she finally opened her eyes, she still felt drained but more serene. This was the first time that Italia had experienced a space that acknowledged the emotional toll of living as an undocumented person and the impossible choices that they had to make.

The rest of the weekend was a blur for Italia. Because the CDN had to elect a new executive board, the organizers dedicated a large part of the next day to explaining the work and the significance of the board. Of particular interest to Italia were the discussions about potential local and statewide campaigns. Even though immigration reform happened at the federal level, state and local officials could pass policies to make life easier for their immigrant constituents. There was the seemingly ever present campaign for driver's licenses for undocumented people and a campaign for state and private financial aid for undocumented college students.[35] They talked about how to push back against the memoranda of understanding between local law enforcement and ICE. This is when Italia felt as if she got her marching orders. These two days weren't just about learning about activism the way she might learn in a classroom; this was about doing advocacy work. At the end of the day, Italia and her peers from SAFE had some ideas about where they might push for better policies not only for undocumented students at RCC but also for immigrants in Riverside in general. As the retreat wound down, Italia was energized and inspired, as well as deep in thought. Her view of the world had been cracked open; she was beginning to see a bigger picture beyond her community. For the first time since she understood what her undocumented status meant, she felt empowered to be part of the efforts to make broad political change. Years later, she would remember this weekend as a moment that changed her life.

Back at RCC, SAFE continued to provide a safe space for undocumented students to be in community with one another and to provide information and resources. Understanding the limitations of the group, Italia believed that the university itself needed to be held accountable for educating undocumented students, including providing adequate student support. Emboldened by her experiences with the CDN, Italia ran for and was elected RCC student body president. In that position, she was part of the conversations to set policies and practices that would make the overall student experience at RCC better. In large part, however, Italia had taken on the responsibility of being student body president so she could advocate for undocumented students as an openly undocumented person herself. She knew that her story and her position made a powerful statement to the campus community. Even though her final year at RCC was marked by seemingly endless meetings and conference calls from early in the morning sometimes until late at night, she was grateful to be doing work that was meaningful, that could make an impact on the lives of future generations of undocumented students.

For both Miguel and Italia, student organizations were critical to the development of their political consciousness. For Miguel, experiences with his UER brothers helped to destigmatize his undocumented status; then PODER placed him in community with other undocumented students and helped him to gain the knowledge, leadership skills, and confidence to begin to advocate for younger generations of undocumented students. For Italia, the academic and civic engagement arms of the Puente Project helped her to understand her status intellectually and opened the possibility of advocacy work around undocumented issues. While the CDN is not a student organization per se, its work with undocumented student organizations across the state were a key part of Italia's political formation, specifically instilling in her a sense of power about the impact that she could have on immigration and education policy. A key part of their political education occurred in student spaces, which illustrates how knowledge is shared and created outside traditional classroom spaces. For Miguel and Italia, this knowledge shaped their legal consciousness and emboldened them to become leaders in their communities.

Shifting Political Contexts

In the spring of 2011, I had been teaching at UC Riverside for almost five years, and in that time I had known several undocumented students, many of whom would confide in me their challenging work situations—driving long distances without licenses to their jobs from campus and back—as well as their anxiety about revealing their status to friends. As a professor of Chicano/a/x studies and a scholar of migration, I made purposeful decisions to include material about how immigration policy rendered a certain part of the migrant community undocumented. In these classes I discussed with my students that illegality was not arbitrary; lawmakers decided which migrants would be legal and which would be illegal. I regularly invited students from PODER to my classes to talk about undocumented student issues. I included this content because I wanted my students to know that that, despite federal legislation over the years that had attempted to fix the perpetually broken immigration system, these were not debates that solely occurred on paper. People's lives continued to be affected by immigration policies that did not match our country's economic needs. Specifically, I wanted my students to see that undocumented immigrants were not always separate from the university. The DREAM Act that had failed to make its way through Congress over the previous decade would have provided a pathway to citizenship for undocumented young people who had been brought to the United States as children by their parents. These were young people who were not much different from them. I wanted my students to understand that immigration policy had an impact on educational access for migrant young people and that some of their peers might be navigating illegality even as they occupied the same classrooms and campus spaces that they did. In short, I considered myself an ally.

When PODER's annual scholarship banquet was announced that spring, I purchased tickets without knowing that the event had spurred local controversy. A local Latino man who promoted his affiliation with the Minutemen, an anti-immigrant vigilante law enforcement group, had publicized the event to his networks, and people were calling the office of the vice-chancellor of student affairs (VCSA) to demand that the banquet be canceled.[36] When it was apparent that the VCSA was not going to cancel the banquet, the Latino Minuteman announced that he would be gathering people to protest. Knowing this in advance, the VCSA coordinated with PODER and campus police to provide campus security at the event.

Not privy to what had been happening in advance of the banquet, I was taken aback by the protesters, whom I could see almost as soon as we pulled into the parking lot closest to the HUB, where the banquet would be held. As my husband set up the stroller for our three-month-old daughter, I took her out of her car seat and laid her gingerly on the passenger seat so I could change her diaper before we headed to campus. I had dressed her in a sleeveless pink sun dress; from past banquets I knew that people dressed up for the event. I was similarly wearing a spring dress, and my husband was in a button down shirt and jeans. We strapped our infant daughter into the stroller, tossed the dirty diaper into the undercarriage, and began walking toward the protesters. There were about a dozen of them, all middle aged and mostly white, though there were also a couple of Latinos in the group. They made their presence known by waving large American flags and holding signs with anti-immigrant slogans. There was a wide enough berth that we could walk to the side of them, but we could still hear them yelling at us that scholarships should be for US citizens; that "illegals" should go home. We were among other small groups of banquet attendees walking from the parking lot to the HUB, noticeable because of our dress clothes and our brown skin. I saw a UC Riverside alumnus walking ahead of us—someone I knew to be undocumented—casting long side looks to the protesters, and I thought that if I felt unsettled as a citizen, he must he feel worse. Now feeling anger surge in my stomach, I resisted the urge to throw the dirty diaper in the direction of the protesters.

Inside the HUB, we approached the receiving table to present our tickets. A tall, broad-shouldered young man with glasses and dark shaggy hair stood behind the students who were taking tickets and checking people in. I recognized him as a student, so I asked him how he was doing. He told me that UC Riverside police officers were outside the HUB, but he was providing another layer of security. We talked a little bit about the protest, but once inside the large room that had been set up for the banquet, the threat felt distant—at least, for us. I was happy to see that the chancellor would be offering remarks of support; the VCSA was also sitting at a table near the stage. The UC Riverside ballet folklórico group performed; dinner was catered by a local taqueria; and we heard various speakers. For me, one of the most powerful but strangest parts of the evening were the undocumented students' testimonios, personal stories that would help banquet attendees understand why their contributions to the PODER scholarship fund were needed and how they might make a difference in the lives of students.[37] The problem was that not all of the undocumented students in PODER wanted to be identified. The group had always promoted itself as being composed of undocumented students *and allies*, which I understood as a way to provide cover to undocumented students who did not want their status known.

When it came time for the testimonios, the organizers dimmed the lights and drew our attention to a large screen set up on a wall to the side of the stage. They used a computer to begin a PowerPoint presentation. Each slide contained the recorded voice of an undocumented student narrating their personal story. There was some text on each slide, but no identifying information— just the disembodied voices. Later I learned that one of the women who had recorded her story for that night's presentation did so because she knew it was important to tell her story, but she was not ready to come out about her status. She held this part of her identity close, not disclosing it even to close friends, many of whom were present that night to support her involvement in PODER. She was dismayed when she heard them trying to figure out to whom each voice might belong.

The rest of the banquet went smoothly. When we filed out of the HUB and back to our cars, the protesters were gone, the sun having set long before. Despite the way it had started, it was a good event, and we were happy to have supported it both financially and by our presence.

Over the next year, as I continued to teach in the areas of education and immigration, I came to know Victor as the new president of PODER. When I invited members of the group to speak to my class, Conditions of Chicano/a Education, in the winter of 2012, he and another group member spent twenty minutes candidly speaking about the support undocumented students needed and the work PODER did and answering my students' questions. I enjoyed talking to Victor; he was confident, smart, and clearly academically driven. I assumed that he was undocumented, but I was never sure, as he was very discreet about his status. I noticed that in his presentation he never spoke personally; he focused primarily on the group and its activities. I didn't yet know how he was leading PODER to be more of a "safe space" for undocumented students or that he was inviting people such as Miguel to join to cultivate their leadership. With the most recent failure of the federal DREAM Act in May 2011 and the dim prospects for federal immigration reform, undocumented students were unsettled, continuing to live their "lives in limbo," many resentful at being used as political pawns in national immigration debates.[38]

As Victor was finding his footing in campus leadership, Italia—also a transfer student from RCC—found herself struggling to manage her schoolwork and the expense of a UC education. The higher tuition and fees had led her to take on two jobs—one at a local taqueria and one at the cellular phone service provider MetroPCS. This meant that she did not have much time to spend on campus. After three years of intense student advocacy and leadership at RCC, she found herself arriving on the UC Riverside campus only for classes and then quickly leaving for work. This changed when she began her second year, in the fall of 2012. She had DACA status, which gave her a two-year temporary work permit, and she was able to apply for financial aid through the California DREAM Act. These two things meant that she could work fewer hours and focus more on school. It was at this point that Italia felt ready to join PODER.

Though Italia and Victor had overlapped during their time at RCC, they met for the first time at a PODER meeting at UC Riverside. It was Victor's first year as a transfer student at UC Riverside, and he was at the meeting as a student; Italia was the student body president at RCC attending the meeting to see about a possible collaboration between SAFE and PODER. When Italia finally had the time and energy to become involved in PODER, Victor was starting his second year as president of the group. She knew that he was invested in being a good leader, but she could see that he was hesitant to push the group toward advocacy. Victor was discreet about his status, and he thought it was important for PODER to be a truly safe space for undocumented students. Public-facing advocacy work might jeopardize students' feeling of safety.

Nevertheless, Italia continued to talk to Victor about how she thought the group could be more innovative and more involved in advocating for state and national policies that would benefit the undocumented community. She would tell him, "The experiences of undocumented students are different than they were before. Before, people were working hard to get their degrees and get out. The priority was education. We have different things now." "Now," she said, "There's deferred action, there's financial aid. Students have the space and want to be more involved. We can't be doing the same things they were doing, like, three years ago or four years ago. We have to do different things." Italia believed that being in college should be about not just education but also what students could do in the process of getting their education to transform society. Students could be involved at different levels: from volunteering to advocacy and protest. She told him, "This could be our way to give back to our communities and our families; to make an impact." Italia knew that Victor wanted to make an impact but that he had reservations about how to balance being public with being safe. At the same time, she knew that he recognized that other members of the group might be willing to do more than they were currently doing. The group was on the brink of change.

PODER Banquet Redux: Pushing through Fear

Two years after the Minutemen protest, Victor asked me to speak at the 2013 PODER banquet; the group thought it would be good for a faculty member to offer their perspective about the situation of undocumented students (figure 3.1).

The banquet felt familiar. There was a silent auction for gift baskets and assorted pieces of art at the back of the room; as in years past, a local group of family musicians, Los Romeros, played traditional Mexican music on acoustic guitars as people filed into the banquet room and during dinner; the caterers from Ojo de Agua, a local taqueria, were also a regular fixture there.

I arrived alone that year and found that the students had seated me at a table with several UC Riverside administrators, including the interim chancellor of the university, Jane Close Conoley, who would be offering

Providing Opportunities, Dreams, & Education in Riverside

KEEPING DREAMS ALIVE
"Raising Dollars for Scholars Banquet"

Thursday, May 2, 2013
University of California, Riverside

3.1 Program for PODER's Spring 2013 scholarship banquet.

welcoming remarks on behalf of the university. This was not new. High-level administrators attended the banquet fairly regularly, usually to offer welcoming comments. Talking to her, I realized that she was not very familiar with the situations of undocumented students, and I was impressed with her desire to stay and learn from them. Her presence and that of the other administrators made me a little nervous because my speech included personal information that I might not necessarily have shared in a professional setting. Specifically, in the speech I included the story of how, two generations earlier, my family had arrived in the United States without legal documentation—at night, crossing the river that divided northern Mexico from South Texas. Most of my remarks, however, recounted the stories of the undocumented students who had crossed my path over the previous seven years. I spoke about those students' financial struggles and the anti-migrant sentiment they sometimes endured both on and off campus.

Immediately after my speech, members of PODER would be delivering their testimonios. In a departure from years past, when this part of the banquet was prerecorded, the students would be speaking live and in person. Because I had been at the other banquets, especially the one that had been protested, I knew that this was significant for them. I felt it acutely when Victor spoke about his family's journey: how he and his mother had overstayed their visa; how she worked as a house cleaner; that he would sometimes join her in that work; his deep frustration at not being able to attend a four-year college right out of high school, even though he had been at the top of his class; his family could not afford the expense. Because I knew how deeply private he was and how closely he guarded his legal status, I appreciated the courage it took for him to tell his story that night.

But even those students I did not know personally delivered deeply moving testimonios. It was Miguel, who came from a small farming community very close to my hometown of Bakersfield, who made the deepest impression on me. Later I learned that Miguel had only grudgingly agreed to give his testimonio that night. He hated public speaking, and he did not usually disclose his legal status to large groups; he felt pressure to speak that night, however, because he was a PODER officer—one of the leaders of the group—and he was graduating. He told me that he had not fully committed to speaking until the day of the banquet, and in order not to overthink it, he had decided to simply jot down a few key points and let them guide the way he would tell his story. He had felt unsettled and nervous all day. To assuage his nerves, Miguel threw himself into the last-minute preparations for the banquet. He helped Victor set up the silent auction. He and other members of the group positioned round wooden tables around the room and covered them with white linens. They arranged centerpieces; they set out the programs for the event. In the couple of hours before the banquet, Miguel went home to change into slacks and a button-down shirt. He combed his hair. Returning to the HUB, he busied himself helping the caterers set up their serving tables; he volunteered to retrieve items from the Office of Chicano Student Programs—a microphone, a roll of duct tape, an extension cord.

As people filed into the large room and the program began, Miguel found himself glancing nervously at the stage. It was a temporary stage that moved a bit and creaked whenever anyone walked up its stairs or from one side to the other. The wooden podium was to one side and had already been set up with a microphone. Feeling a pit in his stomach, Miguel took time to sit with some of his UER brothers to eat dinner.

I must have noticed Miguel along with the other PODER members who were moving the program along, especially as I looked to them for cues about my turn to speak and as they ushered me on and off the stage. But it wasn't until I was back in my seat alongside the chancellor that I really saw him.

Miguel recalled for me an intense nervousness as he looked out at that audience of at least a hundred people, most of whom were unfamiliar to him. He remembered feeling regret that he had agreed to speak, but he also knew that it was too late to back out. He looked at his notes and began to muddle through his talking points. Those first few moments didn't feel authentic to him; he felt as if he was saying things that were expected of him: the generic story of an undocumented youth amplified on a microphone. At one point he looked up from his notes and could see that there were parents—immigrant parents—in the audience. They were women and men dressed in their Sunday best, looking at him the way his own parents might. He thought about how his mom and dad had left their home in Mexico, risking their lives to cross the desert and living under the shadow of illegality for years so he and his sister could have a better life; so they could go to college, earn degrees, work in jobs that wouldn't punish their bodies year and after year. He knew how proud his parents were of him as a college student. He could see that pride in these parents, too. And he knew that he needed to honor those parents' sacrifices with a speech that was true.

Miguel abandoned his notes and began to speak freely about his life over the previous three years. It had been a struggle, especially without financial aid. Things that his peers took for granted, he had either worried about or done without—a driver's license, textbooks, even a bed during his first few months as a student. Miguel's story felt familiar to me because I had heard similar stories from other undocumented students over the years. There was a moment, however, when his voice cracked and I could *feel* the stress—the pain—of living that way. As we all witnessed him begin to weep on the stage, I was reminded that, though this was a common experience, it was also an immensely personal struggle. I looked to the chancellor and saw tears on her face, as well. Some of the students in the audience yelled encouragement to Miguel to keep speaking.

He took an audibly deep breath and continued. He told everyone that he was from a small farm town in the Central Valley outside Bakersfield, where everyone—all the Mexicanos, at least—worked in the fields. This was my moment to feel a lump in my throat. This student was from my part of the world; my parents' and grandparents' generation were also farmworkers. He talked about working in the fields during summers to save money for the following school year.

"You know those cuties that you all like to eat? I picked those."

I understood why he had to make that legible to them. Outside of the Central Valley, most people don't think about where their fruit and vegetables come from. A bag of mandarin oranges—cuties—is simply purchased at a grocery store. When you are from the valley, however, agriculture is the backdrop of your life. You drive along highways and see people in fields hunched over crops that grow low to the ground or standing on ladders in groves of fruit and nut trees. If you are Mexican American from that region, you probably have family who work or have worked in the fields. If you are not from the valley, you might never have to think about it. You might speed past on a highway once or twice and never notice them.

Miguel was a farmworker, and he was a college student.[39] He was poised to graduate and go to law school, where he would focus on immigration law.

I joined everyone who clapped vigorously after Miguel finished speaking. It was rare for me to encounter students from the Central Valley at UC Riverside, and I was disappointed that I had not met him sooner. I tried to approach him, but he was flanked by friends and, I presume, strangers, who were hugging him and congratulating him, telling him what had resonated with them about his speech. Months and even years later, people would remind him of the "cutie" speech that he gave that night. For a long while he was embarrassed that he had cried, that his speech had been so confessional. But eventually he realized what I knew as soon as he finished speaking: that it had been a gift to us all.

Coming to Political Consciousness

As young migrants, Miguel and Italia developed their legal consciousness through experiences in the US school system, developing Mexican American identities alongside peers despite their actual legal status. While this type of segmented assimilation is important to consider among young migrants, Miguel's story illustrates that the fear that his parents felt being incorporated into the context of work powerfully shaped his legal consciousness. That is to say that, even though these two generations of migrants learn how they belong to the United States in different contexts (in this case, school and work), living side by side they inevitably project feelings of fear and stigma onto each other. However, these negative feelings associated with not belonging are not stagnant. Miguel's and Italia's educational trajectories illustrate that this type of "legal consciousness" can radically shift over a few years.

It was within institutions of higher education that Miguel and Italia experienced the most profound changes to their understandings about legality, identity, and the immigration system as a whole. While Italia began to develop a critical consciousness about these issues within a classroom context, it was mostly outside the classroom that both she and Miguel learned the most profound lessons about belonging, dignity, and their own ability to effect social and political change. For Miguel, the Latino brotherhood of the UER and then the undocumented student community of PODER were catalysts that helped him to shed the shame that he felt about his legal status. For Italia, it was the Puente Club, SAFE, and, ultimately, the CDN that facilitated both a critical consciousness and political awakening that empowered her to openly advocate for policies that would benefit the undocumented community. These student organizations were crucial spaces of education for Miguel and Italia that shaped not only their political consciousness, but also their life trajectories. When considering higher education, recognizing these informal spaces of teaching and learning helps us more fully to understand the politicization and empowerment of young people as they begin to claim rights for themselves and to advocate for their communities.

4

UNDOCUMENTED TEACHING

Advocacy and Activism as Pedagogy

It is Cash for College night on a late January evening at Norte Vista High School in Riverside. The sun is setting in shades of purple and orange behind the football field. White stadium lights cast a glare on the lanky players who are finishing their practice. A chill slowly settles into the air as I walk deeper into the campus from the parking lot. Two football coaches in red shorts and white polo shirts point me to the library and resume their conversation as I walk with tepid confidence in the indicated direction. It doesn't take long for me to see a long line of people that snakes around the building that I assume is the library. The families in line are mostly Latinx: girls with ponytails and bright eyes talking animatedly to their friends; boys with dark hair in loose-fitting clothes shuffling their feet, their conversations a murmur; parents with the creased faces of people who have just completed a day's work. Tonight high school staff will help these families fill out the Free Application for Federal Student Aid (FAFSA) application, which the federal government uses to assess students' financial need for college. Fluorescent lights shine brightly through the windows of the library, revealing the volunteers who are preparing computers and adjusting chairs. Because I am a volunteer, I walk toward the front of the line and find that the doors are closed.

I notice an impeccably dressed middle-aged woman with auburn hair walking purposefully around the building, her heels clacking on the concrete. I stop her and tell her that I am a volunteer to help families fill out the California Development, Relief, and Education for Alien Minors (DREAM) Act application. She greets me by pressing her hands to mine in a warm handshake and introduces herself as Mrs. Lomeli. I catch that she is a counselor while she is ushering me around the building. It's dark now, and the stone building is lit solely by the occasional yellow light. Almost as soon as she thanks me for volunteering we find ourselves in a computer lab, where a few parents and their teenage children are already huddled around computer screens. Mrs. Lomeli delivers me to the person who is in charge of this session and promptly disappears. The professional dress of the young woman I am now talking to doesn't make her look older; she seems very close to the age of the students I've seen that night. She tells me that she has just graduated with a master's degree in education from a nearby private university and is working as a substitute teacher at Norte Vista. She is hoping to secure full-time work here. I think she might be volunteering tonight to show her commitment to the school and its students. I appreciate this but wonder why the school has not assigned a full-time staff person to help undocumented families fill out California's new financial aid application for undocumented students. As we talk, she quietly monitors the few students and families who have begun to fill out the application for financial aid through the California DREAM Act. They are largely working independently, and she is unobtrusive. Little by little, more students and families walk quietly through the door and settle around the computers.

I start to think that this will be a quiet and informal event. I had been nervous to volunteer because I knew about the California DREAM Act only as a policy. I didn't feel confident that I could help someone fill out the application. A few days earlier I attended a training, but it only brought anxious memories of filling out the FAFSA decades earlier and, more recently, tax forms. So far, however, it seemed that the students and their families might simply ask for technical support related to the computers in the lab or for help with any unclear questions on the application. Then, about five minutes before the event is officially scheduled to begin, Italia arrives with a few other members of Providing Opportunities, Dreams, and Education in Riverside (PODER). She walks through the door laughing and talking loudly. She sees me and smiles broadly. "Hi, Dr. Nájera," she says.

Now that she is there, I feel like I'm in the right place. She jokes that it feels strange to be on this campus since she graduated from the rival high school across town. Even in her midtwenties, with her faded jeans and T-shirt, she looks like she could be a student at this school. That perception shifts quickly as she invites the PODER volunteers and me to join her at the front of the room.

"Buenas noches," Italia begins in a loud voice.

The families who have been working on the application pause and adjust their seats to give her their attention. Italia proceeds to speak in fluent, though slightly Americanized, Spanish. She thanks everyone, especially the parents, for coming that evening. She introduces herself as a University of California (UC), Riverside, student and tells them that we are here to help them with any questions that they have about the application. She then asks each of the volunteers, including me, to introduce ourselves to the families we will be helping. Following her lead, we introduce ourselves in Spanish. I am the oldest volunteer that evening, very close to the age of the parents in the room. At UC Riverside, I'm a professor, and Italia is a student, but tonight I'm clearly receiving instruction from her. I feel slightly awkward for the substitute teacher who is supposed to be managing this event, but she stands quietly and unbothered in a corner, also listening to this opening presentation. It is clear that Italia is in charge. She is the most knowledgeable person in the room.

Teaching as Activism / Activism as Teaching

The years I spent with undocumented student activists and advocates at UC Riverside made me consider how knowledge circulated in the undocumented community and, more broadly, what that knowledge had to do with education. I was most familiar with undocumented student actions that were large-scale and public-facing, such as the protest against Janet Napolitano's appointment as UC president. As I spent more time with students, however, I realized that the majority of their advocacy work was not protest. Rather, they were engaged in several small-scale educational projects such as Cash for College night at Norte Vista High School. I witnessed students standing in front of classrooms talking to other students, as well as to teachers and administrators, about financial aid for undocumented college students; about Know Your Rights workshops; and about other topics that would help students and families better understand how to navigate college and community life. Some of these were regularly scheduled events for PODER, and others were by invitation. The sociologist Kevin Escudero notes that these "less formal discussion-based spaces have largely been overlooked as key sites of knowledge-production in social movements."[1] I knew these teaching moments were also important to understanding undocumented education. Though they were not as visible to the public as protest, they were a critical way for students to build an empowered undocumented community.

Student leadership was an integral part of these educational projects. As undocumented college students, members of PODER took it upon themselves to learn about education and immigration policies, even as those policies changed under different state and federal administrations. These were not abstract policies to opine about on social media or in classroom discussions. These laws determined the contours of their lives. Students in PODER first sought political knowledge for their own survival, but as they became more informed and confident in that knowledge, they began to act as leaders and as teachers. Paulo Freire asserts that "education must begin with the solution of the teacher-student contradiction, by reconciling the poles of the contradiction so that both are simultaneously teachers *and* students."[2] Student activists resolved that dichotomy time and again as they worked to disseminate their knowledge to the next generation of undocumented students and their families, as well as to campus staff and administrators. This work was radical, humanizing educational praxis motivated by students' desires to create the world in which they wanted to live—a world in which they could be supported by well-informed university staff and administrators; in which undocumented students would feel a greater sense of belonging on campus and less fear.

Community education about immigration issues is an important part of undocumented education because it builds collective knowledge and power. This type of education is closely related to Freire's concept of educational projects. He argues that while systematic education (e.g., the curriculum we see in public schools) "can only be changed by political power," educational projects are carried out "with the oppressed in the process of organizing them."[3] The difference between PODER's educational projects and pedagogies of home or a general kind of public pedagogy is that these projects have the explicit goal of empowering the undocumented immigrant community.

Members of PODER organized and participated in events to circulate information about immigration and education policy. This included updates about federal immigration initiatives, such as Deferred Action for Childhood Arrivals (DACA), in addition to state policies that were relevant to immigrants. Events such as the Cash for College night at Norte Vista High School, for example, shed light on a state educational policy that would make college affordable and accessible for undocumented youth. During the Trump era, members of PODER held Know Your Rights workshops on UC Riverside campus so that, in the case of an immigration raid, students would better understand how to respond and where to find resources.

Undocumented education in these spaces was more than just the dissemination of information. It was a way for undocumented students to assert their humanity, especially in a country that relentlessly dehumanizes them through its policies, practices, and rhetoric. Freire's concept of the pedagogy of the oppressed provides a useful framework to understand this type of educational practice. He states, "The pedagogy of the oppressed . . . must be forged with, not for, the oppressed . . . in the incessant struggle to regain their humanity. This pedagogy makes oppression and its causes objects of reflection by the oppressed, and from that reflection will come their necessary engagement in the struggle for their liberation."[4] Many students in PODER came to political consciousness at their institutions of higher education—at both community colleges and four-year institutions. College contexts opened space for them to learn and reflect on the contradictory and often inhumane immigration policies and practices and to take on leadership roles to push back against micro- and macro-level injustices that the migrant community endured. I understand subsequent undocumented student advocacy and activism as part of the struggle for their liberation. In concrete terms, liberation can mean policy changes. Additionally, students' educational projects help undocumented young people and their families to navigate the United States' dehumanizing legal landscape to live with dignity. Their public-facing educational projects—such as delivering their testimonios—demanded recognition of migrant humanity.

Cash for College Night

A few weeks before that evening at Norte Vista, I was at one of PODER's weekly meetings. That quarter, the group was convening in the evenings in the small lounge area of the Office of Chicano Student Programs. As usual, the members of the group had pushed chairs and worn couches together to make a circle. Toward the beginning of the meeting, Italia announced that there would be a Cash for College night at Norte Vista High School. One of her former Puente counselors, Mrs. Lomeli, had reached out to Italia to ask whether students from PODER could help families with the California DREAM Act application. A few students raised their hands to let her know that they were available. I thought this would be a good opportunity to see how members of PODER engaged the local community and helped to build a pipeline for undocumented students to attend college. I knew that they would let me attend to observe the event, but I also wanted to help. I raised my hand and offered to volunteer. Italia offered to train those of us who had volunteered over the next few days. I would need that training.

A few days before Cash for College night, I returned to the Office of Chicano Student Programs, this time in the middle of the day when students were making their way to and from classes. I arrived before Italia did, and one of the student workers told me I could wait in the conference room. A few minutes later, Italia bustled into the room with arms full of hard copies of the application. Even though the application would be filled out online, she would use the printouts to teach us how to complete it.

"Hi, professor," she said, and she sat down next to me.

Eventually one other person would arrive for the training—a member of PODER who was not undocumented himself, but an ally. Later it occurred to me that other members of PODER already knew how to fill out the application, since they had done it for themselves.

Over the next two hours in that small, windowless conference room, Italia went over each question with us. We talked about what information was needed and what possible answers might be. We discussed questions that people might not be able to answer.

"What if a person does not have an ITIN [individual taxpayer identification] number?"

"They'd just enter zeroes."

Italia knew the answers and how to move forward. I asked her, "How did you learn how to do this?"

"I learned when I had to fill it out for myself watching videos from the California Student Aid Commission.[5] I've done it a few times for myself. And also for my brother."

I left the conference room that afternoon with a tenuous grasp on the application process but knowing that we would be able to figure it out together.

In the computer lab at Norte Vista High School I move around the room with the other volunteers, responding to people who raise their hands with questions. Most students are there with both of their parents, so they are seated in three plastic chairs around one desktop computer. Often I find myself sitting in a fourth chair with families to answer a few questions at once. It's awkward to share such close space with these families as the outsider. More than the space, however, the questions themselves makes the experience feel uncomfortably intimate. Because they are meant to determine students' eligibility for aid and their financial need, several questions ask for personal information. Because the application is in English, the families' sons or daughters and I are translating for the parents, asking about income, savings, and any kind of government assistance they might receive for their children.

For one family:

"Cuánto dinero tiene en su cuenta de ahorros?" (How much money do you have in savings?)

"Tengo $300 en el banco per voy a usarlo para pagar la renta en la semana que viene." (I have $300 in the bank, but I have to use it to pay rent next week.)

For another:

"Cuánto dinero tiene en un cuenta de ahorros?" (How much money do you have in savings?)

"No tengo nada." (I don't have savings.)

"Tiene algo en efectivo?" (Do you have anything in cash?)

"Tengo cinco dólares en mi cartera." (I have $5 in my wallet.)

I feel tension in these exchanges. I don't know how much these parents' children know about the family finances. I recall knowing basically nothing about my own parents' finances when I was their age. But I do catch moments when kids correct their parents, reminding them about income or telling them that they are overestimating an amount.

I am certain that it is difficult to discuss financial matters with a stranger like me. Or maybe I feel tension because of my own class guilt. My salary as a college professor is many times what these families earn each year.

Then there are the questions that go beyond family finances. Has the family experienced problems that might have resulted in an intervention by family court? Are parents separated from children? It's not always clear to me what these types of questions have to do with assessing financial need. These questions seem to speak to family dynamics or family formations, as if they were trying to assess the good character of the family.

After about the first hour, Italia offers clarification for questions about the application that people have repeatedly asked. As if recognizing that the application can be frustrating, she takes time to thank the parents again for coming. She tells them that it is important for them to offer this show of support for their children. Though I know Italia as a student activist at UC Riverside, I try to see her through the eyes of these parents and their high school-age children. She wears little makeup, and her light-brown hair is pulled back into a ponytail, making her look younger than her twenty-four years. Her Spanish is occasionally inflected with an American pronunciation or an English word, like that of other young people who are raised and educated primarily in the United States. She speaks knowledgeably and authoritatively about the process of applying for financial aid and the importance of college. She is expressing gratitude and respect for the parents in the room. I think that she must remind these parents of their own children or—quite possibly—who their children could become if they go on to college.

As the families finish their applications, Italia makes one last announcement on behalf of a sociology graduate student who is also volunteering that night. Signaling to him across the room, she tells the families that he is conducting a research project about the impact of DACA on undocumented youth. She emphasizes how important it is for people like him to do research about our communities so that the government knows what policies are needed. Please help him by participating in his study, she says. As parents and their children tuck their chairs underneath the tables and begin to filter out of the room, I notice that a few approach the graduate student. I say goodbye to Italia and the other volunteers and head home to my family, my mind swimming with everything I've learned that night.

The California DREAM Act dramatically opened access to four-year state universities for undocumented students. Though these students could qualify for in-state tuition if they had attended a California high school for three years, rising tuition costs for public universities were still a barrier. By opening state aid in the form of Cal grants and private scholarships, the California DREAM Act gave undocumented students a viable opportunity to apply for financial aid to attend college.[6] Unfortunately, during the first several months after the act was passed in the fall of 2011, many teachers, high school counselors, and college and university financial aid officers either did not know about its existence or were not sufficiently informed about how to complete the application. The event at Norte Vista in January 2014 occurred just two years after the policy had gone into effect. It is a school that primarily served Latinx students, including immigrants and children of immigrants; its administration thus made the good faith effort to include DREAM Act assistance in its Cash for College night. However, the school didn't necessarily have anyone on staff who was knowledgeable about the application. Both Mrs. Lomeli and the teacher volunteer in the computer lab that night helped to create space for undocumented students and their families. Though well intentioned, they were not well versed about how to complete the application, especially without firsthand experience. Mrs. Lomeli reached out to Italia, knowing that, as an undocumented student and activist, she would probably be in a good position to help.

From the moment she and I met in the Office of Chicano Student Programs through the hours in that computer lab at Norte Vista when she facilitated the session, Italia easily took on the role of teacher. Her training came from what she had learned by seeking the information on her own—through the California Student Aid website and her own experiences going through the process. Given the fact that the only people at the pre-event training were another citizen volunteer and me, I understood that the other PODER volunteers that night had similarly educated themselves about the California DREAM Act. Drawing from the knowledge they had informally acquired, Italia and the other volunteers led the families there that night through the financial aid application process. As daughters and sons of undocumented parents, the PODER volunteers knew how to approach these parents with respect and with appreciation for the work they did for their families. They ran the session entirely in Spanish, which not only created a sense of belonging for parents, but also took the onus off the high school students to translate.[7] As insiders in the community, the PODER volunteers were intimately aware of the situations of undocumented families, including their anxiety, fear, and financial struggles. When, as the lead facilitator, Italia repeatedly thanked parents for participating in the event, she was acknowledging to the parents that, though the application could be difficult and invasive, it was an important step for parents to support their children to move from high school to college. The explicit lessons during Cash for College night were tied to completing the DREAM Act application; however, the implicit lessons for undocumented families were equally important. That evening, undocumented parents learned about college from the example of Italia and the other undocumented college student volunteers. Like their own children, they were undocumented but primarily raised in the United States. With that background, these students stood before them as informed, bilingually articulate young people who were actively giving back to their community.

Though Italia was one of the younger people in the room and had not yet completed her bachelor's degree, she was our teacher. Undocumented students cannot always rely on teachers, counselors, professors, and parents for the information they need to navigate education (and later, job) contexts. When considering undocumented student education, we must consider how those students blur traditional boundaries of authority in the exchange of knowledge.[8] Furthermore, the stakes for Italia and the other PODER volunteers may have been different from those for the school's counselors and administrators: the PODER volunteers could likely see pieces of their high school selves and their parents in the room that night. The California DREAM Act hadn't existed when they were in high school; this was a chance to make things easier for undocumented students and their parents, to help create a world where people like them could be empowered and have access to places that would give them greater mobility.

Dreaming of a Higher Education

On a sun-drenched Saturday in early November, I pulled in to the nearly empty parking lot close to my office on campus to attend that year's Dreaming of a Higher Education conference organized by PODER (figure 4.1). I walked past the boxy concrete building where my office was located and continued uphill toward the science side of campus. The walk was quiet, just the slight rustle of trees with golden leaves and an occasional student walking or riding a bike past me. Approaching a cluster of new, angular buildings with donors' names splashed across their facades, I spotted small groups of people in the distance. As I drew closer, I recognized members of PODER and began to notice parents and teenage students milling around classrooms where concurrent workshops were being held. Student volunteers—members of PODER, but also some from MEChA and UER directed people to classrooms. I smiled and waved at students I knew, then quickly ducked into a session that had already started.

The room stretched horizontally so that the individual desks filled the space from side to side, and there were about a dozen people—parents and their high school-age kids—already seated. They were all turned toward the session facilitator, a longtime counselor I recognized from the UC Riverside Academic Resource Center, Gabe Mendoza. He was presenting in Spanish to the group about what to expect when their children went away to college. I

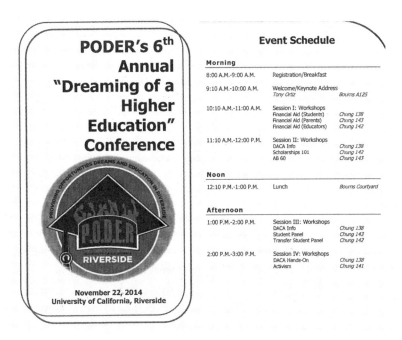

PODER's 6th Annual "Dreaming of a Higher Education" Conference

RIVERSIDE

November 22, 2014
University of California, Riverside

Event Schedule

Morning

8:00 A.M.-9:00 A.M.	Registration/Breakfast	
9:10 A.M.-10:00 A.M.	Welcome/Keynote Address	
	Tony Ortiz	Bourns A125
10:10 A.M.-11:00 A.M.	Session I: Workshops	
	Financial Aid (Students)	Chung 138
	Financial Aid (Parents)	Chung 143
	Financial Aid (Educators)	Chung 142
11:10 A.M.-12:00 P.M.	Session II: Workshops	
	DACA Info	Chung 138
	Scholarships 101	Chung 142
	AB 60	Chung 143

Noon

12:10 P.M.-1:00 P.M.	Lunch	Bourns Courtyard

Afternoon

1:00 P.M.-2:00 P.M.	Session III: Workshops	
	DACA Info	Chung 138
	Student Panel	Chung 143
	Transfer Student Panel	Chung 142
2:00 P.M.-3:00 P.M.	Session IV: Workshops	
	DACA Hands-On	Chung 138
	Activism	Chung 141

4.1   Conference program for PODER's 2014 Dreaming of a
       Higher Education conference.

sat at a desk close to the door and focused my attention on Gabe. He wasn't using the computer console at the front of the room or the whiteboard, but he was clearly engaging everyone in the room, speaking so emphatically at times that his dark wavy hair would fall forward toward his eyes. He told his audience that college students had to be more independent than high schoolers and that students would be responsible for their studies, with less accountability. Nobody would nag them to do their homework. Their professors wouldn't necessarily be taking roll. Students had to learn to prioritize their schoolwork in college. I noticed some students shifting in their seats as he directed comments toward them, some even shyly responding to questions that he posed. The parents—mostly mothers—were rapt, listening and asking questions as if they were the ones who would be navigating college life. Gabe told parents that they shouldn't expect their children to be as present at home as they were in high school, even if they lived nearby. I could see some parents nodding slowly, as if accepting their role—letting go so their children could attain educational success.

Toward the end of the hour, Gabe introduced a UC Riverside alumnus, a young Latino who had been sitting at the edge of the room throughout the presentation. Wearing slacks and a polo shirt with his school's insignia, he looked like a younger version of Gabe. Also speaking in Spanish, he shared with the parents how challenging it had been for him to be the first in his family to attend college. It had been hard for his parents to understand that he couldn't always go home for family gatherings or help in the way he did when he was in high school. Reflecting on this time in his life almost seemed difficult for him, but he spoke deliberately and was respectful of parents. He understood the competing desires for children to go to college while also wanting to keep them close, to keep them safe. He told them that Gabe and other counselors at the Academic Resource Center had helped him find his way, and that he had found strong friendship and support in a Latino student organization he had joined called UER. In other words, their kids would not be alone. He had graduated and was now working as a counselor at a local high school in Riverside. For their part, the parents were not asking him as many questions as they asked Gabe, but they listened to him attentively. He was a decade older than their children, and he had a good job. All of this seemed like a good payoff for a college degree.

Gabe and the counselor ended the session standing side by side, an easy rapport between them. Gabe invited parents to stay behind to ask questions even as the next sessions were slated to begin. A few mothers did stay behind to ask their more specific questions about college life.

As I walked outside, I thought about how important that session was for families of first-generation college students. Though college admissions and affordability loomed large for many undocumented families, Gabe, as a counselor at the Academic Resource Center, was able to address the issues students face once they were on campus as college students. How do families adjust to their children being away from home? How do they continue to support them? How do students create systems of support for themselves when they are away from family? Because UC Riverside serves many first-generation college students, these are questions with which many families and their children grapple.[9] For undocumented students and their families, however, the stakes are higher. Undocumented families often function as a unit. Older children provide childcare for younger children while parents work; sometimes the eldest work to support the family, as well.[10] Parents want their children to have the opportunity to go to college, but they do not necessarily anticipate how the dynamics of the family will shift. Furthermore, undocumented parents worry about their children's safety from immigration authorities. Close to home, parents might feel that they can better protect their children; the farther away they go, though, parents' worries are amplified.

Mulling the particular circumstances of undocumented first-generation students, I walked along the path at the side of the building to another workshop just a few classrooms from Gabe's presentation. "Immigration 101" was being facilitated by the Inland Empire Immigrant Youth Coalition (IEIYC), a regional nonprofit with a mission to empower undocumented youth. I was familiar with the IEIYC, having seen its members at community protests and met young people who were involved in the organization. Unlike PODER, which was composed solely of UC Riverside students, the IEIYC involved young people in the larger Inland community of Southern California, regardless of whether they were enrolled in school. I first heard about the group when PODER students mentioned to me that the IEIYC was hosting a talking circle for undocumented youth. At that moment, when I was at the beginning of my fieldwork, PODER was focused on planning events on campus and actions to push for greater inclusion on campus. The students who had attended the IEIYC talking circles told me that it was really nice to have a space simply to reflect and be in community with other undocumented youth. In addition to those talking circles, the IEIYC was involved in a host of other activities, from community programming to political advocacy.

I walked through the doorway into a classroom that was long and narrow. The same small desks were arranged to face the front of the room, where two young women were working on a computer console. There were more people at this session; about two dozen were already seated. Among them I could see parents and their teenage children, as well as adults wearing T-shirts and polos with school logos, who, I assumed, were teachers or counselors. I chose to sit at one of the few desks remaining in the middle of the room. The murmur of conversations began to fade when the facilitators flipped a switch to lower a screen over the whiteboard.

A few minutes later, the women began their workshop by welcoming everyone—first in English and then in Spanish. The rest of the presentation would follow this format: one presenter would deliver information in English, and the other would communicate the same information in Spanish. Though I knew that they wanted to create a space that was inclusive of both the parents and their kids, this style of presentation made everything feel slower. They told us that they first wanted to talk about immigration policy and cued up a clip from a documentary titled *Immigrants for Sale*, produced by Brave New Films. They lowered the lights, and a blue glow from the projector shone onto the screen that now covered the whiteboard. In that blue light we settled a little more deeply into our seats. Using streamlined, quickly moving graphics, the clip distilled information about how—as privately owned facilities—many detention centers profited from strict immigration laws. The more immigrant bodies spending nights, weeks, and months in detention facilities, the more money the federal government would send to the corporations that owned them. Though interesting to see the connections between immigration law and profitable private prisons, the documentary was sobering. When the presenters turned on the lights, we were left blinking and somber. The presenters asked for questions, but no one raised a hand.

Responding to the silence, the session facilitators abruptly shifted to the second part of their presentation, which was about health care for the undocumented community. They turned the lights down again and started a short video produced by the University of California, Los Angeles (UCLA), Labor Center. It opened on a Latinx family—grandparents and two children—sitting side by side on a couch. The grandmother holds a wooden box in her lap. Speaking directly to the camera, she says that the family's ancestors left something for them that "cures it all," regardless of preexisting health conditions, and that is affordable and accessible to all. The family feigns excitement as the grandmother opens the box to reveal a small blue container of "Vaporu." I could hear low laughter across the classroom, as we all recognized Vicks VapoRub as a commonly used home remedy in Mexican households. The rest of the short documentary presented scenes in which family members experience various ailments—nighttime coughs and stomach pain—that are miraculously cured by rubbing "Vaporu" on the affected areas. The video veers toward the ridiculous as the grandmother character asks her husband to rub it on his head for hair loss (he wakes in the morning with a full head of hair). In another scene around a dinner table, the family applies the ointment to stomachs and chests for diabetes and high cholesterol. Still eliciting laughter from those of us in the session, the clip ends with a series of messages in simple white text on a blue background:

> We can only do so much on our own.
>
> 11 million people in the U.S. are undocumented.
>
> Without papers, many suffer or die from easily treatable conditions.
>
> Health is a human right.[11]

The presenters again turned up the lights and asked for questions. Though the mood was lighter after this presentation, no one raised a hand to ask a question or make a comment. The facilitators ended the session with information about Riverside's Rapid Response Network, which would provide support in the event of an immigration raid. As they passed out small cards with the phone number, I could see several people studying them and placing them carefully in their purses and wallets.

Back outside, I saw Anahí sitting on a large concrete step. Her dark curly hair contrasted against her white T-shirt, and her eyes were fixed at a spot in the distance. I could hear clicking sounds and noticed that she was distractedly pressing miniature buttons and turning small gears on a blue-and-white plastic gadget with one of her hands.

"What's that?" I asked.

"It's kind of like a fidget spinner," she told me sheepishly.

Now a senior, Anahí was one of the co-presidents of PODER. I thought about how much more responsibility she was taking in the group than when I met her as a first-year student.

"What's going on?" I asked.

"There are, like, a hundred a people who registered for the conference who haven't shown up."

"It's still a great turnout."

"Yeah. There are more than two hundred people here, but we planned for three hundred. Now we have all these box lunches that are going to go to waste."

I had been to four or five of these conferences over the previous several years, and of them all, this one was the best attended. I tried to tell Anahí that, but she was still visibly disappointed. She stood up and, still looking away, told me that she was going to help distribute box lunches to conference attendees.

Moments later I stood in line to grab my box lunch, then looked for a place to sit and eat. There were small groups of conference attendees scattered around the main building where the sessions were being held. I chatted with students I already knew, catching up on the quarter and remarking on the turnout for the conference, but mostly enjoying the sun and the mild fall afternoon.

One of the first events that PODER organized was a gathering for undocumented high school students and parents about college. Elias, one of the founding members of the group, recounted to me that PODER hosted the gathering at a community center close to campus. At that moment in the early 2000s, there weren't many resources for undocumented students and their families. The California State Assembly had passed Assembly Bill (AB) 540, which made undocumented students eligible for in-state tuition, but without financial aid college still seemed out of reach for many families.[12] These early members of PODER knew that they were the exceptions in their community, and they wanted to let other students and families know that college was a possibility. Being an undocumented college student was difficult, but it was not impossible.

That year PODER presented information about AB 540, and they invited a trusted local lawyer, Russell Jauregui, to speak to the group about legal protections. The group's members spoke to the families about their own journeys toward and through college. And they met with small groups of parents. Adela, a member of PODER at that time who initially felt a lot of anxiety about leaving Los Angeles for college in Riverside, talked to mothers and assured them that their kids could leave and would most likely be safe. Elias emphasized to me that this all occurred before DACA; before the so-called Morton memos that were intended to deprioritize schools as sites for immigration raids; and before the emergence of the Undocumented and Unafraid movement.[13] Members of PODER were "out" to varying degrees, and many did feel the stress of managing school, but they wanted to reach out to the community to share the information that they had learned along the way.

Within a few years, in 2008, with the help of Chicano/Latino student organizations on campus such as MEChA and UER, PODER began to host its Dreaming of a Higher Education conference on the UC Riverside campus. It invited speakers from different offices on campus—not only the Academic Resource Center, but also the Admissions and Financial Aid offices. The conference always had a keynote speaker—sometimes this person was undocumented, sometimes not—but that person was always meant to inspire students to continue their education after high school, to not let their legal status deter them. In addition, PODER always included a panel of undocumented students who could speak to their everyday experiences and struggles; there was always at least one transfer student on that panel. The workshops have changed to respond to new policies and the political climate. At the first Dreaming of a Higher Education conference, undocumented students had no financial aid options. However, in subsequent years, as new education and immigration policies emerged, PODER included workshops on the California DREAM Act (state aid) and DACA, which, in addition to temporary legal protections, included a work permit. After the Trump administration stopped accepting new DACA applications, the conference stopped offering a DACA workshop, instead prioritizing a Know Your Rights workshop.

Over the years, PODER began to reach out to local high school teachers and counselors to invite them to attend alongside students and parents. One of the frustrations that students expressed to me time and again was that their high school staff did not know how to help them. The best teachers and counselors would look for information, but many did not. For this reason, it was important for members of PODER to use the conference as an opportunity to teach high school staff about the resources that existed for their undocumented students and their possibilities for matriculating at college.

The Dreaming of a Higher Education conference illustrates an important way that undocumented student activists meet a political/educational goal: to broaden access for undocumented students to attend college. As a conference, it is one of the most formal ways that PODER students can disseminate information not just about matriculating at college but about how to navigate college as an undocumented student. The education scholar Tara Yosso defines navigational capital as "the ability to make our way through social institutions not created with Chicanas/os in mind."[14] The university was not created with Latinx students in mind; these students have had to push college administrations to be responsive to their particular needs and to be more inclusive. The Latinx undocumented students navigate issues similar to those of their first-generation counterparts but face additional barriers because of their legal status. Yosso notes that navigational capital is connected to an individual student's resilience, but it also depends on support from other individuals, families, and communities. They initially rely on one another to build resilience and navigational capital; the conference then provides space for them to teach others—families, students, and high school staff—how undocumented students can navigate a university that was not designed for them within a state that criminalizes and threatens them with expulsion.

The other work of the conference—along with providing information—is about shifting peoples' ideologies about who belongs at the university. The presentations by the Academic Resource Center and the IEIYC do the radical work of helping undocumented families imagine their undocumented children as college students and all that entails, even if it means accessing financial aid in a different way or attending college far from home. The information bolsters the idea not only that can they go to college, but that there will be safe space for them there, a space where they can belong.

4.2   Students gather at the center of campus for PODER's Coming Out
of the Shadows event.

Coming Out of the Shadows

The winter sun bore down on the center of campus at midday, and the
shadow of the gray stone bell tower stretched westward. Students from
PODER had set up a dark-blue pop-up canopy for shade next to the tower,
where they would be hosting their Coming Out of the Shadows event (figure
4.2). By the time I arrived, the group had already affixed large, hand-painted
posters to the shady side of the structure that read "Undocumented, Unafraid, Unapologetic" and "Coming Out of the Shadows," punctuated with a
power fist. Students from PODER were testing the sound of the microphone
they would be using; adjusting long, heavy cords; and talking among themselves. I noticed that several of them were wearing white T-shirts with the
image of a hummingbird hovering over barbed wire, with the words "UCR
PODER" underneath. I would learn later that they had made the shirts at a
social event the night before with the help of Dewey Tafoya, a Los Angeles
artist affiliated with Self Help Graphics.[15] Several students were also holding
cardboard cutouts of butterfly wings that were painted in shades of orange,
yellow, and blue (figure 4.3).

4.3   Students with butterfly wings after the Coming Out of the Shadows event. Courtesy of Mafalda Gueta.

After saying a quick hello to the PODER students, I walked to the top of the long concrete steps in front of the tower where several students were already seated, their heavy backpacks positioned to their front and sides. From that vantage point, I also recognized staff and administrators, mostly from divisions of the university related to student affairs, waiting for the event to begin. Because it was noon and we were at the center of campus near the campus eateries, dozens of other students were walking by or riding past the tower on scooters and bicycles, many craning their necks to see what was happening.

Moments later, Mafalda took the microphone, strode toward the center of the crowd, and welcomed us to the event. He started by telling us about PODER as a group whose primary goal was to help undocumented students succeed in higher education. It was February 2016, and most of the undocumented students in PODER had benefited from President Barack Obama's DACA program, which gave them temporary protection from deportation and work permits to help them make ends meet. Obama's presidency had not been perfect—his deportation record earned him the label "deporter-in-chief" from Janet Murguí, the chair of the National Council of La Raza—but nearly 800,000 undocumented young people had received temporary relief from deportation through the DACA program.[16] Now that his presidency was in its last year, however, presidential nominees were asserting themselves on the national stage, including the Republican nominee, Donald Trump. At this point, Trump had gained attention for his dramatically anti-immigrant platform. Despite DACA, Mafalda recognized his community's vulnerability—including the vulnerability of his family. They were living through a hostile political moment when a presidential nominee was talking about building a larger border wall and deporting the eleven million people in the United States without legal documentation.

"I am one of those eleven million people," Mafalda said to the crowd emphatically, not wanting DACA to distinguish him from those who did not meet the program's narrow eligibility standards.

After his introduction, different members of PODER took their place in front of the crowd to share their stories. Jazmin was one of the first student speakers that afternoon. She was wearing jeans, tennis shoes, and that same white T-shirt with the hummingbird hovering over barbed wire. By that point, I knew that she was self-conscious about her slightly accented English, but she began her testimonio speaking confidently, almost forcefully, about her experience. Actually, I realized, she was speaking about her parents' experiences. It was hard for her to see her parents struggle day in and day out in jobs that were "not great." Her mom cleaned hotels and was expected to work quickly, using harsh chemicals. Her dad worked in landscaping, which, she emphasized, had taken a toll on his body.

"My parents are young," she said, "but every time I see them, they look older."

Jazmin's voice echoed across the center of campus and, at times, was a little distorted. She told us that she had also worked in difficult conditions before coming to UC Riverside. She recounted her time working in the agricultural fields around Fresno, where summer harvest temperatures soar past a hundred degrees.

She was holding one of the cardboard cutouts of butterfly wings, pressing it to the front of her body with her arm, while she managed the microphone and its heavy cord with her free hand. She continued by saying that DACA had helped her.[17] She was in school. She had a work permit that gave her access to better jobs. But she reminded us that there were many people who are not eligible for DACA, including her parents.

"That's why I'm here," she stated. To help her family. So that they would not have to continue to sacrifice their bodies for their work.

It felt cathartic when she finished speaking. We applauded as she walked back toward the awning that the PODER students had set up, and several people hugged her. Someone offered her a bottle of water.

That afternoon the testimonios were short, five to ten minutes each, but they were powerful. After Jazmin spoke, another student took the microphone and began to tell her story about being a citizen with undocumented parents. Her experience was markedly different with the protection of citizenship, but her anxiety about her parents' deportability was apparent. She talked about how important it was for citizens to be allies to work on behalf of undocumented communities. The next two speakers—both undocumented women—talked about family separation and their work in school to make their families proud, to make their sacrifices worthwhile.

Alejandro was one of the last speakers that day. He strode to the front of the crowd in a white PODER T-shirt, baggy khaki shorts, and tennis shoes. His black hair was neatly combed back. I noticed that he was shifting his weight back and forth on his feet, thinking he must be nervous as he started to tell his story. He began with his age. He was twenty-eight, an old man on this campus. This testimonio would be about his journey to get to college. He had worked with his father in construction to help his family beginning at twelve, but by eighteen he was ready to work on his own. He started driving without a license. Because he didn't have a Social Security number, he could get jobs only at small family-owned businesses. He recounted that he often earned below minimum wage ($5–$6 an hour) six days a week, ten hours a day, to make his work worth something.

At the same time, he was taking classes at his local community college. But because neither he nor the financial aid counselors knew about AB 540, which would have allowed him to pay in-state tuition, he was paying nonresident fees of $900–$1,000 per semester. He paid for it all out of pocket for years. Being able to fill out the AB 540 fee waiver made a huge difference. He started to work less, focusing more time and energy on school.

"I was in community college for ten years," he asserted. "It took me ten years to get here."

His voice began to break, and he paused, taking a deep breath.

A lump was expanding in my throat as I joined the crowd clapping and cheering him on, wanting him to finish what he needed to say.

"Finally DACA came," he continued. "I finally got a job. A real one. I could finally be proud of who I am. Not just because of work or material possessions. But because I came to school more often. I met people who were super supportive of me. I transferred."

He started to speak more forcefully and with urgency, remembering.

"I didn't know how the hell I was going to afford this shit. I still don't know how the fuck I'm going to afford graduate school. But I'm here. I'm proud. I'm undocumented. I'm fucking educated."

The crowd erupted into loud applause, but he continued to speak into the clamor: "I'm not ashamed of this shit."

He ended by telling us that he was looking forward to continuing his story; to telling it someday to his students, because he was going to be a high school English teacher. He wanted to help other undocumented and first-generation students who weren't yet aware of all they could do with their lives.

"I wanna be their source. I wanna be their light. Just because you don't have a Social or your parents don't know that you can go to college doesn't mean that you can't go."

I was blinking back tears as Alejandro walked back to the awning with the other members of PODER and handed the microphone to Mafalda.

Mafalda's familiar baritone reminded us that we lived in a liberal state where undocumented students paid in-state tuition and were eligible for financial aid. But this issue went beyond students, beyond school. There were millions of undocumented people, he said, who lived their daily lives in the shadows, fearing deportation. He told us that they were taking on the fight for their families so they could all live without fear.

The use of testimonio has a long history in Latin America and among Latina feminist scholars, who have theorized it as a way to narrate collective stories often imbued with political consciousness.[18] In the context of undocumented students, Genevieve Negrón-Gonzales reminds us that "creating and sharing testimonio is a practice of reflecting on one's own life and connecting one's personal experience to a broader social and political context."[19] Connecting personal experience to the broader social and political context reflects political consciousness—reconciling what students learn in classroom settings with what they learn in their families and in their communities. When students act on that knowledge—through the public delivery of their testimonios, for example—they are teaching others about the far-reaching impact of the state on people's lives.[20] The PODER students were teaching others about the real-world impact of immigration and education policies, knowledge that extended beyond what their classmates or professors might learn about in academic books and articles. Often their testimonios stood in contrast to the narratives that circulate about migrants—what the anthropologist Leo Chavez calls the Latino threat narrative.[21] They helped others to see that the undocumented community was diverse, imperfect, and, most important, interconnected.

In addition to teaching, delivering these testimonios in public is a way that PODER students insist on being seen and heard. Negrón-Gonzales emphasizes the ways undocumented student activists use testimonio as a kind of a counter-spectacle. For decades, politicians and media have cast the US-Mexico border as a spectacle to further particular political agendas.[22] Held at the center of campus during the crowded lunch hour, PODER's Coming Out of the Shadows event is a counter-spectacle. Students publicly assert their migration stories on a microphone that resonates across campus. Even those students, university staff, and professors who do not attend the event hear them and may be curious to see them. The students insist that, at least for a moment, people pay attention to the immigration laws that make life difficult and strip them of their humanity. Though students may feel anxiety about publicly asserting their undocumented status (or even public speaking), they used the Coming Out of the Shadows event to push back against the shame and fear that shape the lives of many undocumented people. In particular, the students that day spoke about their families. As the education scholar Susana Muñoz asserts, "Families are central to activists' work, then, as recognition of the injustices that their undocumented parents must bear, parents who, for the most part, continue to live in fear."[23] Members of PODER used that moment to assert their humanity and that of their parents within the immigration system.

For students in PODER, a large part of their advocacy work consisted of small-scale educational projects. In these educational spaces, undocumented students became teachers to their peers and their parents, as well as to school staff and faculty. In these reimagined educational spaces, PODER members shed light on the immigration and education policies that would help expand access to college. In these reimagined educational spaces, they asserted their right to belong and to live with dignity on college campuses and in their communities. By circulating knowledge to others—about policy and about what it meant to live as undocumented people in the United States—they were empowering the migrant community. Building collective power was a way for students to create the world they wanted to live in, a world where migrants could experience less fear, be treated with respect, and push for greater rights.

5

MOBILIZING UNDOCUMENTED EDUCATION

The protest at the Los Angeles Metropolitan Detention Center was not on the agenda. But on the last day of the second University of California (UC) Undocumented Student Summit, UC students who worked with the organizations ICE Out of CA and National Day Laborer Organizing Network invited their peers to participate in the annual "Chant Down the Walls" event in downtown Los Angeles (figure 5.1). It was late April 2016, and Mafalda thought that this year's summit felt different. He had been one of the student protesters who had interrupted UC president Janet Napolitano's opening remarks at the first Undocumented Student Summit the previous year. He had stood alongside representatives from all of the other campuses to call attention to the fact that students had not been part of the planning process for the summit and their suspicions that the newly appointed Na-

Students protest outside the Metropolitan Detention Center
in downtown Los Angeles. Courtesy of Mafalda Gueta.

politano was using the summit to bolster her public image. At this second
convening of undocumented students there were fewer high-profile names
on the agenda, but the conversations among undocumented students were
intimate and powerful. To Mafalda, it seemed more attuned to students'
needs than the Oakland summit had been.

The march—unsanctioned by the UC—would wind through downtown Los Angeles. It was an opportunity that spoke to Mafalda. As part of
a mixed-status family, he saw this protest as parallel to the previous year's
protest in Oakland. At that summit, he and others had marched out of a UC
space to make a point about the meaningful inclusion of undocumented
students. In this moment, Mafalda and his undocumented student peers
had the opportunity to march to a major detention center to draw attention to another part of the undocumented community, another part of the
struggle for migrant rights. Even though organizers made sure that students
from the summit understood there would be risks to participating—police
presence in the streets and Immigration and Customs Enforcement (ICE)
agents at the detention center—Mafalda, along with other students from
the summit, decided to join the march.

Mafalda felt a current of energy as the students gathered on the covered walkway outside the downtown hotel where the summit was being

held. There were at least a hundred students from the summit who would be marching. He lingered near friends from UC Riverside facing the march organizers, who were standing on the street, overcast sky behind them, with megaphones in their hands. They began to chant: "Not one more! Not one more!" Mafalda took out his phone and recorded a quick video—the familiar faces of his friends in PODER, the new friends he had made that weekend holding signs that read "Liberation for All" and "The People United Will Never Be Defeated," the traffic cop and the march organizers ready to direct them into the street. It was just after one in the afternoon when they began to make their way through the heart of downtown Los Angeles, mostly on city sidewalks, marching and chanting as the sun broke through gray clouds.

Mafalda and his peers looked like typical college students. He wore a plain black T-shirt and jeans with blue Converse sneakers and an orange baseball cap. Others wore shirts that bore the names of their universities—Cal, UCSB, UC Merced—or political slogans such as "ICE out of LA." Some were clean-cut and wearing polo shirts; others were tattooed with bright streaks of color through their hair. As they marched, many of their heads were bent over mobile phones, likely sending messages to friends or posting on social media; others were holding their phones high to document the march with photographs and video recordings. Mafalda thought about how different they all were, even as college students. The one thing they had in common was that they were all living without papers. Their families were living without papers.

Marching through the streets that afternoon, Mafalda generally felt safe. In part, this feeling came from the knowledge that he had Deferred Action for Childhood Arrivals (DACA), he was a student at a UC campus, he was a student organizer, and he had a network of people he knew would help him if he was detained.[1] He also knew that he had a backstory with public appeal. He had come to the United States seeking health care; after multiple surgeries and struggles, he had learned to walk. (He was walking through downtown Los Angeles in protest!) Though it had been a struggle for much of his life, in this case he saw his disability as working in his favor. It illustrated the promise of America to help a child in need. Mafalda did take precautions. Per the instructions of the march organizers, he had written the phone number of an immigration attorney on his arm. He shared his phone's location with his partner so they would be able to locate him if he was detained. During the march itself, however, among the waves of students making their way through the streets, he felt safe. More than safe, he felt enveloped by his community. He felt empowered.

Up to that point in his life, Mafalda had been frustrated about his inability to fully participate in the political process. He knew more about political candidates and policies than many of his peers on campus. He was likely more politically informed than most people his age in general. But because he couldn't vote, he never felt fully enfranchised. Without citizenship, he felt shut out of that kind of political engagement. As a student activist at UC Riverside, he knew that he was making change in his own way, especially in terms of helping the needs of undocumented students to be recognized. This moment, however, felt different. He and his undocumented peers were making their voices heard—literally raising their voices in the streets. People were stopping to watch them march by. These bystanders were recording the protest on their phones. He knew that he was probably on a stranger's live social media feed right now. This felt real.

Mafalda and his peers chanted and lifted up their signs:

Estamos Contigo
Families United, Not Divided
We Are Here For You
Free Our Families

Looking around, he could see that some of the protesters were smiling, laughing, and embracing, while others allowed their anger to be manifested, shouting and raising their fists into the bright blue sky. He noticed that his friend Alejandro, also from PODER, was marching with his wife, a University of California, Los Angeles (UCLA), alumna. They were holding a handmade sign that read, "Deport Hate, Not Humans." The largest sign was a banner that read "Undocumented and Unafraid" in wide red letters across a white background that students pressed against the chain-link fence on the Highway 101 overpass. The afternoon sun was beginning to cast long shadows between the buildings downtown as Mafalda and the other protesters arrived at the Metropolitan Detention Center.

He leaned his head back to take in the length of the building. It looked like every other corporate high-rise in downtown Los Angeles. Clad in stucco and several stories high, it was studded with dozens of tiny windows. From this vantage point, Mafalda knew that they were seeing just one piece of a massive building that took up almost the entire city block. Though the area where they would be protesting was closed to traffic, they could hear the hollow roar of passing cars from Highway 101, which flanked the building. Mafalda thought about the hundreds of people who drove by this building every day; how many people might be inching by in traffic without knowing that this nondescript building was a federal prison housing hundreds of migrants detained and awaiting their deportation proceedings.

Mafalda joined his peers in forming a semicircle in front of a short metal fence. He noticed a musician dressed in a long tank top and shorts who had set up in the middle of the street with her small band—a guy sitting on a box drum, a guitarist, someone on a keyboard. As the woman began to sing and rap into her microphone, Mafalda realized that it was Ana Tijoux, a Chilean French hip-hop artist he had learned about from his music-loving dad. The protesters were still chanting at the top of their lungs:

> El pueblo!
> Unido!
> Jamás será vencido!

Now Tijoux's music was being amplified, as well. She was singing a song that sounded familiar to Mafalda. He kept hearing the phrase "sacar la voz" (lift up your voice). In the middle of the noise, Mafalda started to listen, really listen, to the lyrics of the song:

> Sacar la voz que estaba muerta y hacerla orquesta
> Caminar, seguro, libre, sin temor
> Respirar y sacar la voz
> Liberarse de todo el pudor
> Tomar de las riendas, no rendirse al opresor
> Caminar erguido, sin temor
> Respirar y sacar la voz.
>
> Raise up the voice that was dead and make it an orchestra
> Walk confidently, freely, without fear
> Breathe and raise your voice
> Free yourself of all the shame
> Take the reins and don't give in to the oppressor
> Walk confidently and without fear
> Breathe and raise your voice.[2]

Mafalda could feel a knot in his throat, a knot that would appear even years later when he recalled this moment: Tijoux singing "sacar la voz," imploring them to continue to be brave, to be proud of what they were doing that day.

He looked up at the building again, and this time he looked closely into the narrow windows. Though they were tinted, he could make out people's faces. He realized then that the detainees could hear the protesters. Soon they were pressing their hands against their cell windows. Some were pounding on the glass. Then there were small signs made out of what looked like toilet paper, others of old newspapers. Mafalda saw one with a heart drawn on it and a "U." "Love you" was what it said. Another read "Gracias," the letters rolled out top to bottom on toilet paper. He looked around and saw tears streaming down his friends' faces. He knew what they were feeling.

Mafalda thought about his parents; how at any moment—a wrong turn, a missed stop sign—that could be them.

Despite and maybe because of the intensity of the moment, Mafalda and some of the other protesters began to dance when the music turned. Some people were moshing in the streets. They were laughing (some through tears). They were embracing. One of the protesters performed a spoken word poem. Mafalda realized that somehow this was also a celebration of community. They were in this together.

Even after, as he and his friends trickled back to the hotel, he could feel the energy in his body. He called his parents and made another call to his partner—his voice now raspy. He would lose it completely over the next day. He let them know that he was on his way back. He was safe.

The Chant Down the Walls protest was a formative moment in Mafalda's education. He knew the privileges he had as a DACA recipient and as a university student, especially compared with migrants such as his parents, who lived with much more legal precarity. These were lessons he learned as an adolescent, but they became clearer as he became politically involved as an undergraduate at UC Riverside. It was during that part of his education that Mafalda developed a language to talk about how immigration and education policy were manifested in his everyday life. That was also when he realized that he was part of a political community that could affect those policies. While he could more readily see concrete changes on campus and in the UC system, the Chant Down the Walls protest broadened his purview. Chanting and marching through the streets of downtown Los Angeles crystallized for him all of the things that he understood about the immigration system and his family's position in it. He also realized that his political voice could reach beyond the university. In fact, he could use his education and relative legal stability to advocate for migrants who were criminalized by the same system that deemed him "worthy" of DACA's protections.

The action that day was a powerful illustration of one of the ways that knowledge circulates in the undocumented community. By the end of their time as undergraduate students, members of PODER had been immersed in an intense political education. In primary and secondary education they had learned different lessons from parents, schools, peers, and community about what it meant to be undocumented in the United States. In many cases, these were multidirectional flows of knowledge. The young people in PODER did not simply absorb lessons. They reflected and grappled with them. In some cases, they pushed back, and ultimately, they themselves became the purveyors of undocumented knowledge. As PODER students moved through the school system, and especially when they matriculated to college, their understanding of the immigration system and higher education began to shift, sometimes dramatically. In their classrooms they learned about history, culture, and politics from different perspectives. Outside these classrooms they learned how US policies were applied; about political strategies; and, perhaps most important, that even as noncitizens they had the power to push for systemic change. Paulo Freire writes that "liberation is a praxis: the action and reflection of men and women upon their world in order to transform it."[3] Undocumented flows of knowledge were part of this kind of praxis that could lead to social transformation both in and outside of the university.

Though Chant Down the Walls was an emotionally charged event, it was a proactive political action; students were building on their knowledge and smaller political gains. Seven months later, after the presidential election in November 2016, students' political priorities and their praxis would dramatically shift. In the months and years after the election of Donald Trump, members of PODER, along with immigration activists across the country, had to pivot from building on political gains to both defending the pro-migrant policies that they had won and pushing back against new, aggressive anti-immigrant legislation. Beginning in January 2017, the president used his executive power to try to ban migration from certain Muslim-majority countries, allocate money for a more robust border wall, expand the capacity of ICE to conduct immigration raids, and, eventually, attempt to end the DACA program. The specter of deportation began to loom more heavily in students' lives—if not for them, given the uncertainty of DACA, likely for their parents.

This chapter reflects a different branch of undocumented education. Circulating knowledge and information was more critical than ever during the Trump administration. PODER students had the political knowledge and skills to do the increasingly important work of migrant advocacy in this politically hostile context. They were also consistently working to change common ideologies about the migrant community that were circulating in the public. They had access to information and had built the critical skills to parse through the political noise about the new administration. They worked with others to understand the limits of Trump's power, and they tried to abate people's fear with information. They worked with immigration attorneys and continued to disseminate information to their communities so they would know their rights. They pushed the university administration for responses to what was happening on the federal level; built new coalitions on campus with other students who were affected by the new right-wing administration; and increasingly took their work to the streets in the form of off-campus public protests.

For undocumented students in PODER, community building was equally important to, if not more important than, this urgent educational work. While in many ways it was a privilege to be a student, it was now also an acute responsibility—one that placed them under immense emotional strain. Creating, maintaining, and being present in undocumented safe spaces helped to anchor students to understand that they were not alone; that other young people were in the same situation; and that they had allies. From the time Trump was elected through the four years of his presidency, there were no easy answers or solutions to his administration's barrage of anti-migrant policies and practices, what some scholars refer to as "legal violence."[4] However, these moments in community with other undocumented students and allies gave students a safe space to express their humanity, including their feelings of frustration and fear. These occasions provided a reprieve from the dehumanizing rhetoric and policies of the Trump administration, giving students a rest from their public roles as activists and community advocates. Students knew they were not really undocumented and unafraid, but they were brave. And they knew with certainty that they and their families deserved to be treated with dignity.

Education and the Struggle for Migrant Rights

On November 8, 2016, Donald Trump was elected president of the United States. For more than a year before his election, he campaigned on a platform that was anti-immigrant, promising to build a wall between the United States and Mexico; characterizing Mexican immigrants as drug dealers, criminals, and rapists; and announcing that he would ban migration from Muslim-majority countries.[5] PODER students and other students with migrants in their families and communities might have felt protected from some of these proposals in California. Undocumented students would continue to have access to in-state tuition and state financial aid. All undocumented migrants in the state were eligible for driver's licenses. Within the year, the California state legislature would pass Senate Bill (SB) 54 to declare California a sanctuary state that would prohibit state agencies from cooperating with ICE.[6] In other words, living in a state controlled by Democrats offered some protections from new, restrictive federal policies. Nevertheless, the election destabilized much of the security that students had begun to feel on the UC Riverside campus.[7]

The impact of the election was not lost on the UC administration. Less than twenty-four hours after the presidential election had been called for Trump, UC president Janet Napolitano issued a statement about the university system's commitment to its values of diversity and inclusion and its stance against intolerance:

From: *Faculty on behalf of James E Grant Jr*

Date: *Wednesday, November 9, 2016 at 11:52 a.m.*

To: *Staff, Students, Faculty*

Subject: *[Faculty] An important message from President Napolitano and UC Chancellors about yesterday's election results*

President Janet Napolitano and the Chancellors of the University of California today (Nov. 9) issued the following statement:

In light of yesterday's election results, we know there is understandable consternation and uncertainty among members of the University of California community. The University of California is proud of being a diverse and welcoming place for students, faculty, and staff with a wide range of backgrounds, experiences and perspectives. Diversity is central to our mission. We remain absolutely committed to supporting all members of our community and adhering to UC's Principles Against Intolerance. As the Principles make clear, the University "strives to foster an environment in which all are included" and "all are given an equal opportunity to learn and explore." The University of California will continue to pursue and protect these principles now and in the future, and urges our students, faculty, staff, and all others associated with the University to do so as well.

We are proud of what the University of California stands for and
hope to convey that positive message to others in our state and nation.

This was the first of several emails from the UC administration at the system-wide and campus levels that contained statements of support for vulnerable students and provided information about their legal rights and university resources. At UC Riverside, the three-year-old Office of Undocumented Student Programs (USP) took on an even more important role of disseminating information about students' and families' rights and local resources. Continuing its work, PODER increasingly focused on providing information and creating safe spaces for undocumented students who were grappling with the implications of Trump's impending presidency, as an email announcing the November 15 talking circle shows:

From: *PODER at UCR*

Date: *Monday, November 14, 2016 at 10:48 p.m.*

To:

Subject: *PODER General Meeting 11/15*

Hello Folks,

I hope you all had a restful three day weekend! As you all know post-election season has brought many uncertainties. And now more now than ever we will continue to create a safe space and educate our community. That being said, we invite you to join us as we grie[ve], heal, and build together. This Tuesday 11/15 we will be hosting a talking circle moderated by a campus counselor, at Chicano Student Programs from 5:00–7:00 p.m.

Additionally, Undocumented Student Programs will be hosting a workshop, "Immigration Info session" presented by an attorney from UC student legal services, to discuss immigration outcomes after elections and answer questions, Nov. 17 from 1 p.m.–3 p.m.

Undocumented Student Programs talking circles had become part of the office's regular programming, usually offered at midday and providing food for students. I had attended some of these talking circles over the previous year but was not there for the one held the day after the election. I ran into Alejandro on campus a couple of days later. We checked in with each other about how we were feeling, and I asked him whether he had gone to the talking circle that week. He had. He told me that it had felt like a funeral. "It was like we were all gathered around a dead body," he said. I understood what he meant. The shock and grief were almost palpable during those first few days after the election. But the image of the dead body was also apt. It was as if the movement PODER students were building—everything that they had worked for—was now lying inanimate at their feet.

Campus always looks different at night, everything in shades of gray. The large trees rooted on the perfectly partitioned lawns cast tangled shadows under the moon and lamplight. Only the occasional student walks or cycles along the pathways. From where I park it is a short, brisk walk to the Office of Chicano Student Programs, where I have attended dozens of meetings with students over the years. Fluorescent lights glow through the office windows. I notice a hand-painted sign propped against one of the windows whose red lettering reads "Viva La Raza." It has been almost six months since I've attended a regular PODER meeting; I've been trying to devote myself to writing up what I have already learned from the group. But tonight I want to show my solidarity with students.

Members of PODER have made the most of the small space, pushing together worn couches and chairs to form a circle. On the main wall is a bright mural of a brown-skinned woman standing at the front of a line of faceless bodies, each a different color—orange, purple, red, green, blue—with their hands reaching toward the sky. The woman's arms are muscular, and she is holding up a red flag with a black eagle in the center, the same one that the United Farm Workers introduced when they formed their union to fight for farmworkers' rights in the mid-1960s. In the background the skeletal figure of an eagle looms, an orange sun blazing behind it. Several students are already seated as I situate myself to face the mural. Though I recognize some PODER members, there are also students I have not met. They might be regular members of the group, but I know that the announcement for the talking circle was sent to a listserv that included many students who had attended only a single meeting or signed up to receive information at some point. Andrea Saavedra, a counselor from the university's Office of Counseling and Psychological Services (CAPS), welcomed people as they trickled in.

Andrea had become a familiar face to me over the previous few months. One of the first actions of the Office of Undocumented Student Programs was to reach out to various campus offices to offer workshops and trainings about the unique situations of undocumented students. The CAPS office was of particular importance because undocumented students often struggled to explain the larger structural issues that affected their mental health. Some counselors viewed immigration as an abstract political issue and were not trained to understand how the threat of deportation and family separation, for example, might affect students' mental health.[8] Andrea had attended one of the USP training sessions and immediately made herself available to the USP office as a CAPS liaison. Her own background as the child of undocumented parents made her particularly attuned to these students' struggles and needs. As a liaison, she would facilitate talking circles, and in general, students knew that she was someone they could go to in CAPS who would understand the larger context of their situation. And she would be empathetic.

That night, after several students were seated and quietly talking among themselves, Andrea introduced herself and opened the session by inviting students to express any concerns or feelings that had emerged for them since the election. There was just a brief moment before the first student spoke, and then several students began to talk, building on one another's comments. They were grappling with the same thoughts and worries. One young woman expressed disbelief that people viewed her and her family as criminals. Many in the circle murmured sympathetically and nodded. Students expressed having lived in the United States for years, trying to live by its rules. They felt as if they could not afford to misstep or to make mistakes; they never wanted to jeopardize their place in this country or place their parents at risk. Gaining admission to a UC school, often as the first generation in their families to attend college, was proof of this. Ultimately, being so-called perfect immigrants didn't seem to matter. With half of the country voting for the brazenly anti-migrant presidential candidate, students felt rejected by their adopted country. They felt betrayed.

Students conveyed uncertainty about their future in the United States. Some of their parents were making contingency plans to return to their hometowns in Mexico. While this seemed like a viable option for their parents, it was difficult for students to imagine such a move. Many had no memories of Mexico. Most had left as young children and—without papers—had not been able to return. They wondered what it would be like to return to a place that was completely unfamiliar to them. There was also the possibility that parents would go to Mexico (voluntarily or involuntarily) and their adult children would stay in the United States. What, then, would happen to the children—siblings—who were not yet adults? Would they leave with their parents or stay with their older, college-attending siblings? Many wanted to stay.

Then there was the question of DACA. The program existed because of an executive order by President Obama. Without congressional approval, it was impermanent. Given Trump's stance on immigration issues, many wondered about the future of the program. If DACA were eliminated, their temporary legal protection from deportation would expire, as would their work permits. They would graduate from college and be ineligible for any kind of above-the-table employment.

What struck me that night was that there were no answers. People leaned forward in their seats at moments to listen more intently. They nodded their heads affirmatively and sympathetically. Andrea facilitated the talking circle by asking probing questions and by validating their concerns. In doing so, she created room for students to express their feelings of hurt and their anxieties about the future. No one knew what would actually happen. It might not be as bad as people feared; it might be worse. The only thing that students could take comfort in that night was knowing that they were not alone.

After four years, the protections of DACA seemed normal. Even though President Obama was not as progressive as many had hoped he would be, activists felt as if they could push him for more. The Trump election felt like a major regression, putting everything that had seemed stable on shifting ground. It was the beginning of a new political era, and it was a dramatic lesson in the ebbs and flows of the political movement for migrants' rights.

The election fell in the middle of the ten-week quarter and the end of fall, when daylight waned earlier and brittle leaves began to litter the campus walkways. Those first days and weeks were marked by quiet grief and anxiety. Students were trying to stay focused on their coursework as midterms passed and finals week loomed. I was a member of a private Facebook group that PODER used to make in-house announcements, and I began to notice frequent posts about Know Your Rights sessions and webinars. These were sponsored by national, regional, and local organizations, including the UC immigration attorney assigned to the UC Riverside campus.[9] The group used the Facebook page as well as the listserv to invite students to local organizing events to prepare for the incoming administration's likely anti-immigrant policies; more immediately, there was talk of making UC Riverside a sanctuary campus. At the same time, many of PODER's activities continued as normal. The group was setting up its table at the bell tower on Wednesdays to recruit new members; its members were presenting about their college experiences at local high schools and sharing information about scholarship opportunities. The group hosted an end-of-the-quarter potluck during the last regular meeting of the quarter; PODER had to continue to move forward. There had to be some sense of normalcy.

El Pueblo Unido, Jamás Será Vencido

The new quarter began just days after the new year. The events and activities organized by PODER kept the rhythm of a typical school year. The PODER leadership sent out emails reminding members about meetings; announcing plans for Immigrant Awareness Week, which it hosted each winter quarter; and inviting volunteers to the Coming Out of the Shadows event at the bell tower.

The date of the inauguration loomed.

January 20, 2017, fell on a Friday.

That afternoon I participated in a panel presentation hosted by UC Riverside's History Department about Mexicans and the making of the United States. Later that day, I saw that Mafalda had posted an announcement inviting students to the USP office to make signs for the next day's protest.

That protest was the Women's March, a mass mobilization in different cities across the country to draw attention to women's rights, especially because many of the new president's policy proposals would threaten reproductive rights. The following day in downtown Riverside, I didn't see any PODER students among the sea of pink caps and T-shirts with feminist slogans, but I could see from the group's social media posts that students had participated in protests in Los Angeles and Riverside. They marched alongside family members—mostly mothers and siblings—holding signs. "They tried to bury us. They didn't know we were seeds." I thought they must have felt the way I did after the action that day: buoyed by the feeling of community, with an incredible cross-section of communities coming together. It was a moment of hope.

Then came the executive orders.

The Wednesday after the inauguration, just days after the Women's March, the president issued two executive orders that would shape immigration policy without the approval of Congress. The first was to build a border wall replete with additional US Border Patrol agents.[10] The second was to increase the number of ICE agents by ten thousand, a 50 percent increase, and to withhold federal funds from government entities that provided sanctuary to undocumented migrants.[11] Both orders mandated that the Secretary of Homeland Security work with state and local governments to mobilize Section 287(g) of the Immigration and Nationality Act to authorize state and local law enforcement to aid in the detention and deportation of migrants.[12]

Dread mounted that, with heightened numbers of ICE agents, massive immigration raids were imminent.

Local organizers from Riverside acted quickly, calling on the City Commission to declare Riverside a sanctuary city. The PODER social media sites encouraged students to begin phone banking, calling the mayor's office to voice their support for sanctuary.

That same week, the new administration issued another executive order, this one targeting refugees and travelers from certain Muslim-majority countries. The order suspended the US Refugee Admissions Program for 120 days and the admission of Syrian refugees indefinitely. Another major piece of the order blocked visitors from seven countries, all of which had Muslim majorities.[13] One of the major pain points of the executive order was that it initially prohibited green card holders from those countries from returning to the United States.[14]

Students began to talk more about the contingency plans that their parents were making. How much would it actually cost to move all of a family's belongings to a house in Mexico? If the Department of Homeland Security (DHS) could ban green card holders from entering the country, what chance did they have of someday normalizing their status? The PODER students with DACA considered the implications of living in a country that didn't want them. Did they really want to be college-educated but unable to work in their field of study? Would they end up working in under-the-table jobs to make ends meet while living with the fear that this might be the day they are deported? Was that living?

Within days I saw a post on social media by Guadalupe, the co-president of PODER that year. I had gotten to know her well over her two-and-a-half years on campus. She grew up undocumented in a nearby agricultural community and had been tracked to go to a high school outside of her community, where she would participate in a special International Baccalaureate (IB) program. It was jarring for Guadalupe, as a working-class student, to study alongside so many wealthy young people. After her father's depor-

 January 30, 2017 · ⚮

I am unapologetically undocumented. The President of the United States has issued a ban on all incoming refugees for 7 predominantly Muslim countries. (Even some green card holders are being denied treatment). We all have exams this week.. but some of your fellow Highlanders and UC brethren have family members directly affected by this and family who can no longer enter the country. If you care about me or my fellow Muslim or Middle Eastern students, join us at the Belltower tomorrow in our demonstration in solidarity from 12-2PM. Media will be present. Admin will be present, Truth will be present, will you?

TUE, JAN 31, 2017
UCR Students Against Muslim Ban and Wall
Riverside

★ Interested ⌄

5.2　　Facebook post proclaiming solidarity between undocumented students and Muslim students affected by the Trump administration.

tation, she acutely understood her family's economic and legal instability, even after he made his way back to California. She applied to UC Riverside on her own, informing her parents that she would be leaving for college just months before she was set to move. She had figured out how she would pay tuition, where she would live, and how to enroll on her own. Not surprisingly, once she arrived at UC Riverside, Guadalupe became a leader in PODER and was a vocal advocate for undocumented students.

Guadalupe's Facebook post was part declaration of her status as undocumented, part statement of solidarity, and an invitation to a joint protest sponsored by the UC Riverside Muslim Student Association (figure 5.2). She wrote:

> I am unapologetically undocumented. The President of the United States has issued a ban on all incoming refugees for 7 predominantly

Muslim countries. (Even some green card holders are being denied [entrance]). We all have exams this week . . . but some of your fellow Highlanders and UC brethren have family members directly affected by this and family who can no longer enter the country. If you care about me or my fellow Muslim and Middle Eastern students, join us at the Belltower tomorrow in our demonstration in solidarity from 12–2PM. Media will be present. Admin will be present, Truth will be present, will you?

January 31, 2017, fell on a Tuesday. I walked quickly from the lecture that I had just finished for my Introduction to Chicano/a Studies class to the center of campus, along with a wave of students who were all heading to their next classes or to grab a bite to eat. There was already a small but growing crowd assembled around the bell tower. I could hear chanting led by someone on a bullhorn: "From Palestine to Mexico, border walls have got to go!"

Compared with the Coming Out of the Shadows events I'd attended in this same spot over the years, the students that day were much more diverse. The PODER events primarily drew Latinx and sometimes Asian American undergraduate students. This day, in addition to Latinx and Asian students, there were Middle Eastern, Black, and White students, both undergraduates and graduate students. Soon at least two hundred people had gathered, many holding handwritten signs with slogans such as "No Ban, No Wall" and "Equality for All."

I could see Guadalupe at the front with other student organizers. The crowd quieted for a moment while a young Middle Eastern male student offered a prayer. Another student spoke about how these policies affected them all and the importance of solidarity. Between speakers and spirited chants, Guadalupe grabbed the bullhorn. "I've never had to find myself being with [the Muslim] community and standing in solidarity with them," she said. "It made me think that it sucks that it has to come down to this sometimes . . . for us to be this united."

The protesters began to move from the center of campus, sign and banners in hand. They filed through the first floor of the Highlander Union Building (HUB), where many of their peers were standing in line for lunch. From there they marched under the mild winter sun in their T-shirts and jeans, some women wearing hijabs, others with their hair loose, young men with prayer shawls wrapped around their shoulders, a few waving the Palestinian flag. They stopped at the flagpole at the side of the university administrative building where the chancellor's office was located, chanting, "No hate, no fear, refugees are welcome here."[15]

The demonstration at UC Riverside was one of many that occurred across dozens of California colleges and universities. I saw images from several UC schools of non-Muslim students joining their Muslim peers in prayer at many of these actions before processing through their campuses and local communities. This was in conjunction with images of lawyers camping out inside major airports writing petitions for people arriving from the seven barred countries and protesters outside. While chaotic, the very public nature of these actions and protests drew the attention of migrant communities to one another. Muslim students learned about the border wall executive action the same week that undocumented students learned about the travel ban. The administration's anti-migrant actions were indiscriminate.

During their time as undergraduate students, many members of PODER had come to political consciousness first by understanding that they were not alone in their experiences. There were other students who lived with legal and financial precarity. Being in community with other undocumented students often gave them the confidence to act together; to claim the rights that they did have; and to advocate for the next generation of undocumented students who wanted to attend college. During this moment of relentless anti-migrant policy, undocumented students and Muslim students began to see their connections more fully. Kevin Escudero's "identity mobilization model" aptly describes this kind of coalition building, whereby different groups leverage their intersecting experiences to form coalitions.[16] The cross-community organization was a new political strategy for PODER. Its collective public protest, mounted in the middle of the day that moved through the middle of campus through major campus thoroughfares and the chancellor's office, demanded attention to off-campus policies that were affecting their lives as students. They were teaching the campus community about the immediate human impact of "bans and walls." They were also pushing back against the state, undocumented students publicly signaling that they were not going back into the shadows.

The protests and lawsuits had an impact. That interpretation of the order was quickly reversed, but in the administration's revised executive order, the ban on travelers who were citizens of six Muslim-majority countries remained intact.[17] These actions also created cross-community connections that were important to undocumented student activists at PODER. However, outward demonstrations of strength and solidarity were only part of the story. The Trump administration continued to wield its power, this time through immigration raids.

USP and UC Office of Immigrant Legal Services were indispensable at this moment. The institutionalization of services for undocumented students were the direct result of student activism, particularly in 2013, when Napolitano was appointed president of the nine-campus UC system. Undocumented students and students from mixed-status families could trust the Office of Immigrant Legal Services for legal advice and legal representation for themselves or immediate family members. USP regularly disseminated reliable information about policies, campus responses, and resources available to students, such as this email:

From: *USP STAFF*

Date: *Friday, February 10, 2017 at 9:35 a.m.*

To:

Subject: *UPDATE from Undocumented Student Programs*

Hi Colleagues,

The message below was sent to students about the reported raids in SoCal.

Students,

In light of reports that ICE is conducting raids throughout Southern California (including Van Nuys, Downey, Norwalk, Oxnard, San Bernardino, and Santa Paula), we are sending the attached statement to you all. We do not have any additional information right now, but when we do, we will notify you.

We know this is a frightening and uncertain time, and we continue to be available to support you and your campus communities. We have two scheduled workshops:

Know Your Rights: Protect Yourself. Protect Your Family

Presented by ACLU

Learn how to best interact with law and immigration enforcement, regardless of immigration status, at home or in public.

Tues. 2/21 | 3 P.M.–5 P.M. | HUB 379

Immigration Law Information for Families

Presented by UC Undocumented Student Legal Services

Learn more information on "Green Card through Family" (spouse, parents, siblings)

Thurs. 2/23 | 12:30pm–1:30pm | HUB 279
*As a reminder you can pick up **red cards** from our office.*

Meanwhile, PODER proceeded with its winter quarter programming, including weekly meetings to be in community with one another and to plan Immigrant Awareness Week. In the time leading up to Immigrant Awareness Week, the group launched a social media campaign, inviting students and other members of the campus community to "demystify stereotypes" of immigrants. This involved taking pictures holding signs with pro-immigrant captions and posting them on social media accounts. While some of these would circulate solely on social media, others would be part of a public display at the student union during Immigrant Awareness Week. Next to hand-drawn posters with information about PODER and USP, there were a series of photos of students holding signs in their own handwriting with messages about immigrants that they wanted their fellow students to read. In one photo, a dark-haired, bearded male student in a black Adidas jacket held a sign that pointedly read, "I have never blown anything up." Other examples included

> A curly-haired woman with her head cocked slightly to the side, who smiled broadly and held the message, "If Mexico isn't sending their best . . . Why am I here?"

> A thin, clean-shaven male student with his hair dipping slightly into his eye, wearing a collared button-down shirt and jacket and holding a sign that read, "We don't all look the same!"

> Another woman with long wavy hair and deep-set eyes looking directly into the camera with a matter-of-fact expression and a sign that read, "Immigrants are not uneducated."

> A male student wearing a zipped-up gray hoodie pulled over his head, a smile on his face as he tightly held a sign written in purple marker

just under his chin that said, "Stop dividing us between good and bad immigrants. We're all worthy and we're all #Heretostay."

The display PODER mounted that week was meant to teach others on campus about the immigration landscape—its policies and its ideologies. The group shared information about rights and resources for migrant students and families. For other students, the display of students with their messages helped to create a counter-ideology about migrants. The display was meant to demystify stereotypes, but it also alluded to the pain that such stereotypes engendered among students.

The programming that week—as in previous years—was meant to teach the campus community about what it meant to be undocumented in the United States. That year, however, the group was more intentional about complicating the immigrant narrative, including a session about undocumented and queer identities and continuing to forge cross-community connections through a discussion about Palestinian displacement. The most public event of the week would still be PODER's Coming Out of the Shadows event at the bell tower. In the middle of that week, news began to circulate that a DACA recipient had been arrested and detained outside Seattle.[18] Because DACA was an Obama-era executive order, so-called DA-CAmented students and allies knew that the program was vulnerable. This person's arrest made the program appear even more tenuous, and the events of Immigrant Awareness Week seemed to take on more urgency given the political moment. PODER students continued the programming throughout the week, but this arrest cast a shadow over their work on campus.

At the end of February, as students were entering the last two weeks before final exams, the director of USP sent a message with the subject line: "Social Media Rumors about Homeland Security at UC [Riverside]." In it she included a screenshot alleging that a DHS vehicle was parked in a UC Riverside parking lot, and that this sighting had been "confirmed by staff." The director assured students in the email that she had reached out to the UC Police Department to confirm the sighting, but that no federal agency vehicle was present. She included in the message a guide on how to share reports of raids responsibly on social media.

The push and the pull of those months was exhausting. Undocumented students and their allies were organizing among themselves and with other communities. They were pushing for UC Riverside to become a sanctuary campus, for Riverside to become a sanctuary city. They were pressuring the university administration to take public stances in support of migrant students and their families, and university administrators were voicing their commitment to "diversity," including UC students from migrant families. However, even in a liberal state such as California, in a university system that provided resources to undocumented students and their families, undocumented students felt deeply unsettled.

Undocumented education included the lessons that parents and communities had taught the young people in PODER. These undocumented pedagogies of home had instilled in many of the young people values, work ethics, and knowledge about how to navigate their "illegality." In spaces of higher education, undocumented education was peer- and community-based education that had helped students understand immigration and education policies, their rights, and their ability to bring about change. Students in PODER ultimately became purveyors of undocumented education, disseminating critical information about immigrants' rights and resources to their families, communities, peers, and university staff and faculty. Perhaps most important, students taught others about the meaning and the impact of immigration policy on the everyday lives of migrants. During the Trump administration, undocumented students in PODER continued to do this work not only through educational projects, but also through counter-spectacles meant to draw attention to and humanize the targets of Trump's anti-migrant policies. The work was urgent but emotionally taxing, and there was no end in sight. The students continued to move forward with their activist work, leaning on their communities—PODER, the UC Undocumented Coalition, friends and family—for support along the way.

In May, toward the end of the spring quarter, I attended a midday talking circle sponsored by the USP. The office's staff had reserved a general-purpose room on the third floor of the student union for the event. They had arranged the spindly legged blue chairs in a circle, setting up a table in the corner of the room with sandwiches, chips, and beverages. Two of the room's walls consisted of floor-to-ceiling windows that let in warm afternoon light from the open walkways. Though PODER students were among the ten or so students there that day, the conversation was not oriented toward politics or policies. What struck me were the students' expressions of pain because of experiences with their own mixed-status extended families—experiences with cousins, aunts, and uncles who looked down on them because they didn't have papers. Especially within this anti-immigrant context, rejection by family members was particularly hurtful.

Guadalupe arrived late to the talking circle, grabbed a sandwich, and sat at the edge of the group, eating her lunch quietly and listening. The hour came to an end, and as students began to file out of the room, I went up to her to say hello. Since the No Ban, No Wall protest, I had seen her a number of times, and it seemed that she was always busy. As co-president of PODER, Guadalupe was one of the primary faces I saw at protests. I knew that she was also one of the UC Riverside representatives for the UC-wide Undocumented Student Coalition. Her name was often attached to students' petitions to the administration, and, of course, she was regularly sending messages and posting announcements to PODER members about upcoming events and resources for undocumented students. I told her that I admired all the advocacy work that she was doing.

By now it was just the two of us in the room. She looked at me, tilted her head slightly, and said, "Sometimes I don't feel undocumented and unafraid, you know?"

I thought about the social media posts and public pronouncements that she had made to the contrary, and I nodded.

"But what else can I do? I just have to keep moving forward."

I could see that she was pushing herself to move through the fear of this moment. They all were. Guadalupe, like some of her peers in PODER, had already lived through the deportation of a parent. As a young child she had joined her mother at English-language night classes. When she was growing up in the Coachella Valley, her parents worked various jobs, ranging from construction to gardening. As a sociology major, Guadalupe could talk about labor exploitation; she could also understand her experience at the wealthy high school she attended through the lens of racial and class disparity. She had learned how to be a better organizer alongside student activists such as Mafalda. She was paying these lessons forward as a leader in PODER by advocating for her community both on and off campus. Guadalupe was scared sometimes; she got tired. She knew that her peers did, too. But what helped her—what helped all of them—to keep moving forward was knowing that they were together. They were learning; they were teaching; they were building community. They were imagining and trying to create a world where they could all live with dignity.

EPILOGUE

Here to Stay

Jazmin's graduation cap and gown was hanging on her bedroom door the entire week before Raza Graduation. These were her last weeks as a student at UC Riverside, and she had nearly completed all of the coursework for her applied mathematics major. When she awoke with pangs of dread about the final exams and assignments she had to complete, Jazmin would glance up at that simple black gown and the mortarboard that she had decorated, and she felt the excitement again. The knowledge that she would soon be the first in her family to graduate from college was thrilling. "I'm graduating," she'd whisper to herself. "I'm graduating."

Jazmin had not always been certain that she would make it. She had struggled with some of her early coursework and had been placed on academic probation. She knew that this was in part because of the more rigorous nature of university coursework, but her academic performance was also tied to her ability to pay for college. She had received financial aid through the DREAM Act, but sometimes it was still difficult to make ends meet—to buy books and course materials, food. It wasn't until the summer before her junior year that she realized that she was eligible to apply for DACA. With DACA she was able to work to better support herself. She had been involved in student organizations, including PODER since her first year at UC Riverside, which helped her feel as if she had a place on campus. But it was with DACA and the financial stability that her job gave her that everything, especially her academics, began to fall into place. It had been a winding path through college, but now that her time at UC Riverside was almost over, she was grateful.

On the day of Raza Graduation, Jazmin had everything planned out. Her parents and siblings would be driving in from the central coast, and her grandmother, along with aunts and uncles, would be driving down from the Central Valley. Estimating the hour that they would arrive, she planned enough time to carefully curl her long hair and perfect her makeup. She had chosen a pink dress to wear under her graduation gown, which she had laid out along with the new heels she had bought for the occasion.

Jazmin would participate in three graduation ceremonies over the last few weeks of the quarter. The first was the senior ceremony for the Office of Undocumented Student Programs (USP); the second was Raza Graduation; and the third was the commencement for the College of Natural and Agricultural Sciences (CNAS). Jazmin knew that, because of the distance and expense of travel, her family would be able to attend only one of these ceremonies. The USP graduation would be intimate, but it wouldn't have the pomp and circumstance of a big graduation. Though the CNAS commencement in many ways was the "official" graduation ceremony, with professors in their regalia and university administrators delivering speeches intended to inspire, Jazmin thought it would be more meaningful for her family to attend Raza Graduation.

Sponsored by the Office of Chicano Student Programs and organized by a small group of graduating Latinx seniors, Raza Grad was a bilingual and bicultural ceremony meant to be inclusive of students' families. A key tradition of Raza Grad was for graduates to walk into the ceremony flanked by two people the student wanted to honor. Often it was their parents, but students could choose to take anyone who had been a primary part of their community of care. Jazmin would be walking between her mom and dad.

It had been a hard year for them all. Jazmin's parents had divorced during her senior year of college. In the middle of this family strain, she had given serious consideration to moving home to help with her younger sister and brother. Jazmin thought that, if she were to stop, she could always return to finish and graduate a year late. Her academic adviser—a good one among a revolving set of counselors during her time at UC Riverside—encouraged her to stay. "You're so close," he had said. "There's nothing you can do about [the issues at home]. Just keep moving forward." This day Jazmin was happy that she had heeded his advice. Things were tense between her parents, but her graduation gave their family dynamic some levity, even if just for that day.

Her parents arrived separately, her mother in an elegant black dress with gold jewelry and her father in a suit and tie. When she saw them, her eyes welled with tears. *We're from a rancho*, she thought. *I wouldn't have been able to do this if we had stayed at that rancho, if we had stayed in our country*. She wouldn't have been able to give them this experience, this moment. The hugs and saludos with her parents, younger sister and brother—also elegantly dressed—tías, tíos, and her grandmother were a joyous whirlwind. Anxious for them to experience the festivities, Jazmin quickly ushered them back into their cars and toward campus.

They parked in a large lot next to the track and soccer fields and walked under the already warm sun toward the student recreation center, where Raza Grad would be held. She could see her peers emerging from their cars with their families, many carrying blue, white, and yellow balloons and flowers, their graduation gowns still unzipped and revealing their carefully chosen dresses and suits. Vendors selling bright flower leis had positioned themselves along the path. When they arrived at the rec center complex, families were standing in line to enter, and Jazmin could hear Spanish-language folk and popular music playing inside. She helped her extended family take their place in that line so they could be seated with the general public. Meanwhile, she and her parents entered the lounge of an adjacent building, where they would wait alongside the other graduates and their families.

Staff from the Office of Chicano Student Programs and volunteers were corralling them, giving instructions about the procession amid the happy chaos—the sea of caps and gowns, sashes, purple floral leis, blue and gold balloons, and cell-phone cameras capturing the moment. It was the most fun Jazmin ever had waiting in a line, and it was beautiful for her to see the parents and families of her friends and community members. A fellow math major, a nontraditional student in her fifties, introduced Jazmin to her children, who were the same age as most of the other graduates. Jazmin introduced her parents to her peers and their parents in Spanish and English. In between the animated chatter, she would catch glimpses of her parents, who were looking at her and smiling. Holding that eye contact, she would smile back broadly, not knowing what to say. She hoped they knew that this was for them. It was because of them.

When it was their turn to enter the rec center, Jazmin locked elbows with her parents and walked through the doors. The music that had been muffled from the other room was now booming loudly in her ears along with the noise of conversations and cheers from family members and friends in the audience. The smell of tacos dorados permeated the entrance to the room, and Jazmin was glad that the Raza Grad committee had decided to provide food to the families and friends who were there that day. Looking up and around, everything seemed broad and bright. On her left, family members and friends—from very young to very old—were sitting on bleachers that had been pulled out for the event. She knew her grandmother, aunts, uncles, and siblings were in that crowd. To her right were rows of white folding chairs reserved for close family and friends, and in front of that were seats for the graduates. There was a large, elevated stage draped in blue and gold decorations flanked by enormous speakers. Jumbo screens on each side of the stage were projecting a long PowerPoint presentation highlighting each graduate that day, their senior pictures, names, and majors. On another screen, she caught a glimpse of herself and her parents as they processed toward the seating area. This, she knew, would be live-streamed for people watching from the overflow area and for those who were not able to attend the ceremony in person.

As she walked alongside her parents down the aisle toward their seats, Jazmin thought about the moments that had brought her there. She remembered crying in a bathroom near a lecture hall after getting a bad grade on a test. She pictured herself on the train, tired and looking out the window as she headed to the coast to visit her parents. She caught a glimpse of Mafalda in the audience and thought about the evenings they had spent in the crowded lounge of the Office of Chicano Student Programs, planning the next PODER event. She saw staff who had helped her come up with funds for books when money was tight. And then she was back in the present, walking alongside her parents. There were many times in her life when she was reminded that she did not have papers, and there would be many more of those instances to come, but in that moment, with her family and peers and her community, she felt unmitigated joy.

Jazmin hugged her parents, then went to sit with her peers. She looked down at the sashes that she had chosen to wear over her graduation gown: the blue-toned serape for Raza Grad, the blue UC Riverside sash with gold lettering that read Class of 2017, the pink sash of her Latina sorority, and the PODER sash. These had been her communities at UC Riverside. The ceremony was a happy blur until a staff member motioned for her row to line up on the side of the stage. She heard her name and major amplified across the rec center and approached one of the standing microphones on the stage. She would be given thirty seconds to speak. Jazmin thanked her family for being there, and even though she didn't know whether her family in Mexico would be able to watch the graduation, she gave a shout out to her "familia del rancho de Guanajuato." She wanted everyone in that auditorium to know that the little girl who used to play in the soil of that rancho was now graduating from college.

Exhaling, she smiled broadly, took her certificate of graduation, and strode off the stage, applause resounding in her ears.

This was a moment she knew that she would not forget. Up to that moment, Jazmin had filled her life with short-term goals: graduate high school; get into college; graduate with a bachelor's degree. Because of her status and the uncertainty that it brought to her life and the life of her family, she never felt as if she could plan for the long term. At her graduation, however, she stopped. She realized that she was more than her status and that she deserved more. Yes, she was closing a chapter of her life. Yes, the political situation of migrants was worse than she'd ever experienced. But she considered the older generations of undocumented migrants and thought: *If they made it without DACA, then we can keep going.* Especially looking around at this wave of graduates, so many of whom were migrants and from migrant families, she knew that they were building something (figure E.1). With their college degrees they could help one another; they could advocate for their communities. She was the first in her family to graduate with a college degree, but she wouldn't be the last.

A couple of weeks before Raza Graduation, Jazmin had gotten together with a friend to decorate the mortarboards of their graduation caps. It would be a study break and something to encourage them as they made the final push toward the end of their final quarter. They brought rhinestones in assorted shapes and colors, fabric pens, and silk flowers. Jazmin set to

E.1 Graduating students stand to applaud their parents at UC Riverside's Raza Graduation.

work studding the edges of her cap with the light blue jewels, settling on blue flowers on top and cascading down the back of the mortarboard. She thought about the words that she would write. There was so much that she could say: "For my family"; "First, but not last." She chose the phrase that felt most appropriate for where she was at that moment in her life: "Lo que se siente como el final es a veces el comienzo."

What feels like the end is sometimes the beginning.

Introduction. Undocumented Education

1   Unless noted otherwise, all of the names of undocumented individuals in this book are pseudonyms.

2   Gordon, "Napolitano Commits Funds to Aid UC Students Who Entered US Illegally."

3   See also Cabrera, "Disrupting Diversity."

4   Mafalda is not a pseudonym.

5   Cabrera, "Disrupting Diversity," 80.

6   Ramirez Resendiz, "Subjectivity Making in Undocumented Student Organizing," 45.

7   Alonso Bejarano et al., *Decolonizing Ethnography*; Smith, *Decolonizing Methodologies*.

8   Ábrego and Negrón-Gonzales, *We Are Not Dreamers*.

9   Speed, "At the Crossroads of Human Rights and Anthropology."

10   Sepúlveda, "Toward a Pedagogy of Acompañamiento," 71.

11   Sepúlveda, "Toward a Pedagogy of Acompañamiento," 559.

12   In her work with Oaxacan philharmonic bands, Xóchitl Chávez asserts that accompaniment with the Oaxaqueño community created the kind of trust that enabled bringing the bands to the university space. Chávez, "La Sierra de Juárez en Riverside."

13   Alonso Bejarano et al., *Decolonizing Ethnography*.

14   Hale, "What Is Activist Research?"; Speed, "At the Crossroads of Human Rights and Anthropology."

15   Geertz, *The Interpretation of Cultures*.

16   See Behar and Gordon, *Women Writing Culture*; Visweswaran, *Fictions of Feminist Ethnography*.

17   Bernal, "Learning and Living Pedagogies of the Home."

18   Richman, "Undocumented Students Disrupt Janet Napolitano's Speech at UC Summit."

Chapter 1. The Original Dreamers

1   Nájera, "Remembering Migrant Life."

2   Negrón-Gonzales et al., "Introduction: Immigrant Latina/o Youth and Illegality."

3   Negrón-Gonzales et al., "Introduction: Immigrant Latina/o Youth and Illegality," 7.

4   De Genova, "Migrant 'Illegality,'" 425.

5   Ngai, *Impossible Subjects*; Salinas, *Managed Migrations*.

6   Chavez, *The Latino Threat*.

7   It is important to note that the Dreamer profile was part of a political strategy to achieve piecemeal immigration reform. For an excellent history of the trajectory of the term *Dreamer*, see Ábrego and Negrón-Gonzales, *We Are Not Dreamers*.

8   Nicholls, *The DREAMers*.

9   Nájera, *The Borderlands of Race*.

10   This young woman was not alone in this sentiment. Many young people disagreed with this political strategy, and by 2010, the youth-led aspect of the movement became outwardly more inclusive of undocumented people who did not fit the initial Dreamer profile.

11   In the spring of 2021, President Joe Biden ordered US immigration enforcement agencies to cease using the phrase "illegal alien." Rose, "Immigration Agencies Ordered Not to Use Term 'Illegal Alien' under New Biden Policy."

12   Enriquez, *Of Love and Papers*, 7.

13   Minian, *Undocumented Lives*.

14   Inda, *Targeting Immigrants*; Minian, *Undocumented Lives*.

15   Durand and Massey, "The Costs of Contradiction"; Inda, *Targeting Immigrants*.

16   De Leon, *The Land of Open Graves*; Urrea, *The Devil's Highway*.

17   See Jonathan Inda's compelling work on the rationale/knowledge base behind these machinations of border control. Inda, *Targeting Immigrants*.

18   Cornelius, "Death at the Border"; Inda, *Targeting Immigrants*.

19   The distinction between a political boundary and a politicized boundary

became even more stark after the terrorist attacks of September 11, 2001. See Chavez, *The Latino Threat*.

20   Cornelius, "Death at the Border"; Inda, *Targeting Immigrants*.

21   Today border militarization also includes the practice of long-term migrant detention, following a US Supreme Court decision in 2003 that upheld the right of the government to detain migrants during deportation proceedings and President George W. Bush's 2008 Secure Communities initiative.

22   Cornelius, "Death at the Border"; Kulish, "What It Costs to Be Smuggled across the US Border."

23   Kulish, "What It Costs to Be Smuggled across the US Border."

24   Urrea, *The Devil's Highway*.

25   Quoted in Cornelius, "Death at the Border," 675. The INS ceased to exist after Congress passed the Homeland Security Act in 2002. Its successor, ICE, took on the immigration enforcement role the INS previously had.

26   De Leon, *The Land of Open Graves*; Martinez et al., "Migrant Deaths in Southern Arizona"; Rosas, *Barrio Libre*.

27   Urrea, *The Devil's Highway*.

28   Rosas, *Barrio Libre*.

29   This phenomenon is similar to what the sociologist Leisy Ábrego describes among Salvadoran families. See Ábrego, *Sacrificing Families*.

30   A study by the Pew Research Center found that two-thirds of all undocumented immigrant adults in 2017 had been in the United States for more than ten years, compared with 41 percent ten years earlier. In other words, rather than keeping migrants out of the United States, the fortification of the border has trapped migrants inside the country, dramatically altering the pattern of circular migration that characterized Mexican migration prior to the 1990s. Krogstad et al., "Five Facts about Illegal Immigration in the US."

31   In her book about migrant girls, Lilia Soto writes about how migrant subjectivities—age and gender in particular—shape the experience of migration. Preteen and teen migrants experience the anxieties of both arriving at a new place and perhaps permanently leaving a place behind. Soto, *Girlhood in the Borderlands*.

32   The lack of such a program is likely because of Proposition 227, which eliminated bilingual education in the State of California in 1998. HoSang, *Racial Propositions*.

33   Pérez, *Americans by Heart*.

34   Advancement via Individual Determination (AVID) is a nonprofit organization that trains educators and partners with schools to provide equitable opportunities for working class and first generation students in kindergarten through grade 12. See AVID, "What AVID Is."

35   This was a common experience in the period before DACA was passed

in 2012. Many young people realized the significance of their legal status when they began to approach the markers of adulthood (e.g., applying for a driver's license, applying to colleges, trying to gain employment).

36 "California Nonresident Tuition Exemption," Assembly Bill 540 (October 12, 2001).

37 Ábrego, "Legal Consciousness of Undocumented Latinos."

38 Gabe Mendoza, telephone conversation with the author, August 15, 2021.

39 Sergio's economically motivated decision to return to Mexico aligns with a report from the Pew Research Center that found that, in the years around the 2008 US recession, Mexican migrants were increasingly returning to Mexico. Passel et al., "Net Migration from Mexico Falls to Zero."

40 This legislation was, in part, the result of "Dream activism," wherein young people staged public protests that highlighted the particular circumstances of their undocumented status. Often wearing their graduation caps and gowns and engaging in civil disobedience, they highlighted an immigration system that allowed them access to school but left them with no place to go after graduation. Dream activism reflected a piecemeal approach to immigration reform, sometimes as part of larger, comprehensive immigration legislation proposals and sometimes as standalone demands for legislation. Ábrego and Negrón-Gonzales, *We Are Not Dreamers.*

41 US Senate, "DREAM Act of 2007," S. 2205, 110th Cong. (2007–2008), https://www.congress.gov/bill/110th-congress/senate-bill/2205.

42 The Barry M. Goldwater Air Force Range in southwestern Arizona occupies 2.7 million acres across Maricopa, Pima, and Yuma counties. It is used by the Air Force and the Marine Corps for military training; it is also used as a bombing range. Arizona Department of Environmental Quality, "Barry M. Goldwater Range-East"; Urrea, *The Devil's Highway.*

43 The UC Undocumented Student Coalition, which was composed of at least one student representative from each campus, was formed after the summit. Ábrego and Negrón-Gonzales, *We Are Not Dreamers.*

Chapter 2. Undocumented Pedagogies of Home

1 Jazmin's experience of migration mirrors the experiences of the young women in Lilia Soto's *Girlhood in the Borderlands.* Waiting for family reunification and not having agency over when it occurred was a common theme for the teenage participants in her study.

2 Zavella, *I'm Neither Here nor There.*

3 Roberto Gonzales notes that undocumented students experience divergent opportunities based on the way that they are tracked in the school system. Gonzales, *Lives in Limbo.*

4   Nájera, "Remembering Migrant Life."

5   Bernal, "Learning and Living Pedagogies of the Home," 624.

6   Yosso, *Critical Race Counterstories along the Chicana, Chicano Educational Pipeline.*

7   Cecilia Ayón and David Becerra present a dramatic example of undocumented migrant constraints in the context of Arizona during an era of economic downturn and anti-immigrant policies in 2010. Ayón and Becerra, "Mexican Immigrant Families under Siege."

8   See Enriquez et al., *Entre Familia.*

9   Cruz, "The Union within the Union"; Garcia, "Labor, Migration, and Social Justice in the Age of the Grape Boycott."

10   Genevieve Negrón-Gonzales writes about the financial precarity of undocumented families in the Central Valley and the central role of the labor of youth to a family's financial stability. See Negrón-Gonzales, "Constrained Inclusion."

11   Their family's work situation exemplifies Zavella's concept of the working poor. The wages that Jazmin's parents earned were too low to give them economic stability, especially in coastal California, where the cost of living is among the highest in the nation. Zavella, *I'm Neither Here nor There.*

12   City News Service, "Riverside Border Patrol Office to Close."

13   Laura Enriquez and her colleagues also detail the financial gaps undocumented students experience even with state financial aid and the instrumental role university staff can play to connect undocumented students to resources they need to continue in school. See Enriquez et al., "Mediating Illegality."

14   Undocumented student organizations can help to facilitate a stronger sense of belonging to the greater campus community. See, e.g., the case studies in Nájera, "Creating Safe Space for Undocumented Students"; Santa-Ramirez, "A Sense of Belonging."

15   Minian, *Undocumented Lives.*

16   Carpio, *Collisions at the Crossroads.*

17   De Lara, *Inland Shift.*

18   Maxson et al., "Can Civil Gang Injunctions Change Communities?"

19   Sahagun, "LA Gangs, Drugs Invade Inland Empire."

20   Estrada, "Growing Up in San Bernardino."

21   Years later, in 2013, California passed Assembly Bill 60, which directed the Department of Motor Vehicles to issues driver's licenses to eligible California residents regardless of immigration status.

22   Carpio et al., "Right to the Suburb?"

23   This MOU was made possible by Section 287(g) of the Immigration and Nationality Act.

24   Gonzales, *Reform without Justice.*

25 In Mexico and other Latin American countries, a *notario publico* is a trained legal expert whose qualifications extend beyond that of US notaries.

26 I wrote Mafalda's story primarily based on interviews, but I also drew from Eileen Truax's *How Does It Feel to Be Unwanted?*, which features a chapter about Mafalda and his family.

27 Mafalda is transgender and uses the pronouns he/him/his.

28 HoSang, *Racial Propositions*.

29 HoSang, *Racial Propositions*.

30 Ballotpedia, "Arizona SB 1070."

31 There is an emerging literature about Latinx undocumented students with disabilities. According to a review of this literature by Carlos Lavín and Grace Francis, many studies indicate the barriers and discrimination that families face because of schools' perceptions of them as non-English-dominant migrants, not necessarily because of the children's legal status. Legal status does affect how parents navigate school bureaucracy, taking precautions to remain safe. Recent work by Elizabeth Farfán-Santos provides a compelling and detailed account of the ways that language and legal status dovetail to hinder undocumented families' ability to access resources and services that are meant for low-income children with disabilities. See Lavín and Francis, "Looking in the Shadows"; Farfán-Santos, *Undocumented Motherhood*.

Chapter 3. Undocumented Learning and Political Consciousness

1 According to the California master plan for higher education, the University of California was to be the state's primary academic research institution, and its mandate is to admit the top one-eighth of the state's high school graduates. "Institutional Research and Academic Planning."

2 California State Assembly Bill (AB) 540 allowed undocumented students who had attended a California high school for three years to pay in-state tuition if they signed an affidavit swearing that, if given the opportunity, they would become citizens.

3 "IGETC."

4 A 2020 survey of 1,277 undocumented college students attending public universities in California revealed that 29 percent had participated in an organization to solve a social problem, compared with 19 percent in a 2006 national survey of young people. Enriquez et al., "Persisting Inequalities and Paths Forward."

5 William Rosales and his colleagues find that perceived threat to family spurs political engagement among undocumented students, particularly those students with DACA protections. Rosales et al., "Politically Excluded, Undocu-engaged."

6   The term *1.5 generation* refers to the generation of immigrants who were born in another country but have spent most of their childhood in the United States.

7   In the landmark case *Plyler v. Doe* (1982), the US Supreme Court ruled that public schools may not deny immigrant children a free education based on their legal status. This decision did not address the question of college.

8   Roberto Gonzales compellingly writes about how, after years of being acculturated as American in the US school system, undocumented young people have to learn to be "illegal" when they enter the workforce or matriculate at college. Gonzales, "Learning to Be Illegal."

9   Marcelo Suárez-Orozco and his colleagues found that undocumented young people in the United States have significantly higher levels of anxiety than national norms. Suárez-Orozco et al., "In the Shadows of the Ivory Tower." More recently, the UC Promise study found similarly high levels of stress and anxiety among undocumented young people in California colleges and universities. Enriquez et al., "Persisting Inequalities and Paths Forward."

10   Enriquez et al., "Advancing Equity for Undocumented Students and Students from Mixed-Status Families at the University of California."

11   Because undocumented children cannot be barred from K–12 schools, they are full members of school society, unlike their parents, who are "illegal" in many public and government realms. Seif, "'Unapologetic and Unafraid.'"

12   Freire, *Pedagogy of the Oppressed*.

13   Yosso, *Critical Race Counterstories along the Chicana, Chicano Educational Pipeline*.

14   Nájera, "Creating Safe Space for Undocumented Students."

15   Daniel Solórzano and his colleagues write that colleges and universities with positive campus racial climates typically include four elements: (1) diverse students, faculty, staff, and administrators; (2) opportunities for students to access culturally relevant curricula; (3) programs that focus on the recruitment, retention, and graduation of students of color; and (4) an institutional mission that includes a commitment to diversity. In the absence of one or more of these elements on campus, students forge their own safe spaces. Sólorzano et al., "Critical Race Theory, Racial Microaggressions, and Campus Racial Climate."

16   Nájera, "Creating Safe Space for Undocumented Students"; Rosaldo, *Culture and Truth*; Yosso, *Critical Race Counterstories along the Chicana, Chicano Educational Pipeline*.

17   Yosso, *Critical Race Counterstories along the Chicana, Chicano Educational Pipeline*.

18   Italia is not a pseudonym.

19   Laura Rendón writes that the Puente program has a successful community college transfer rate because it validates students' existing knowledge and academic identities through its curriculum and instructor pedagogy. Rendón, "Community College Puente."

20   MEChA is a student organization that emerged during the Chicano/a movement meant to educate and empower the Chicano/a community.

21   Christine Sleeter posits that ethnic studies courses such as Italia's English course offered through Puente provide the opportunity for students to develop "an academic identity that links to, rather than conflicts with, their ethnic identity." Sleeter, "The Academic and Social Value of Ethnic Studies."

22   The immigration scholar Douglas Massey notes that, after the border-militarization initiatives of the mid-1990s and the subsequent expense and dangers of border crossing, migrants from Mexico were more likely to remain in the United States and to send for their families to join them. Massey, "Immigration Policy Mismatches and Counterproductive Outcomes."

23   Freire, *Pedagogy of the Oppressed*, 83.

24   Freire, *Pedagogy of the Oppressed*, 83.

25   This iteration of PODER is similar to the model students in North Texas initiated, focused on what Mariela Nuñez-Janes and Mario Ovalle refer to as *convivencia* and organic activism. Nuñez-Janes and Ovalle, "Organic Activists."

26   While Stella Flores found that in-state tuition policies increased access to college for undocumented people, Syeda Raza and her colleagues found that in-state tuition alone did not alleviate the financial obstacles for undocumented students in California colleges and universities. See Flores, "State Dream Acts"; Raza et al., "Interrupting the Cycle of Worrying."

27   Enriquez, "Because We Feel the Pressure and We Also Feel the Support."

28   Coalition for Humane Immigrant Rights, "Mission and History."

29   Garcia, "Cesar Chavez and the United Farm Workers Movement."

30   Maria Rodriguez is not a pseudonym.

31   Archibold, "US Plans Border 'Surge' against Any Drug Wars."

32   Melody Klingenfuss, statewide organizer, California Dream Network, conversation with the author, December 2020.

33   Introduced to Congress in 2001, the federal Development, Relief, and Education for Alien Minors (DREAM) Act would have provided a pathway to citizenship for certain undocumented young people who were brought to the United States by their parents. Despite being proposed in slightly different versions over several years, the DREAM Act failed to pass both houses of Congress. See Olivares, "Renewing the Dream."

34   Genevieve Negrón-Gonzales argues that undocumented activists "walk a fine line, trying not to perpetuate a parent-child dichotomy while si-

multaneously arguing for their own rights on the basis of their identity as immigrant students." Negrón-Gonzales, "Undocumented Youth Activism as Counter-spectacle," 102.

35 In 2011, California Assembly Bills 130 and 131, together known as the California Dream Act, made undocumented California high school graduates eligible for financial aid. Two years later, in 2013, California Assembly Bill 60, the Safe and Responsible Drivers Act, made undocumented migrants eligible to apply for driver's licenses.

36 The Minutemen were part of a vigilante law enforcement group that was founded in 2005 to patrol the US-Mexico border, often with arms and other military-type equipment. Though their paramilitary activities mostly occurred at the border, they were also known to protest and intimidate undocumented migrants in nonborder communities. Chavez, *The Latino Threat*.

37 By *testimonio*, I mean first-person accounts of events that have social or political significance and often reflect the perspectives of everyday people whose experiences resonate with, and are reflective of, larger communities. See Nájera, "Remembering Migrant Life."

38 Drawn from the concept advanced in Gonzales, *Lives in Limbo*.

39 Negrón-Gonzales writes about the unique challenges of undocumented youth from the Central Valley whose unique experiences navigating illegality, poverty, and racism lead to what she terms "constrained inclusion." Negrón-Gonzales, "Constrained Inclusion."

Chapter 4. Undocumented Teaching

1 Escudero, *Organizing While Undocumented*, 26.
2 Freire, *Pedagogy of the Oppressed*, 72.
3 Freire, *Pedagogy of the Oppressed*, 54.
4 Freire, *Pedagogy of the Oppressed*, 48.
5 The California Student Aid Commission is a state agency that administers financial aid for students who attend college in California. Its central mission is to make post-high-school education "financially accessible to all Californians." California Student Aid Commission, "About the California Student Aid Commission."
6 For the impact of in-state tuition policies and state financial aid, see Flores, "State Dream Acts"; Raza et al., "Interrupting the Cycle of Worrying." Even with such aid, and especially among students without DACA, undocumented college students continue to experience financial precarity, including food insecurity. See Vazquez Vera et al., *Struggling*.
7 While scholars have made the case that child translating or language brokering is a sign of giftedness, the literature also points to the complex impact language brokering has on child translators and parents. Corona

et al., "A Qualitative Analysis of What Latino Parents and Adolescents Think and Feel about Language Brokering"; Valdés et al., "A Performance Team."

8 Freire, *Pedagogy of the Oppressed*; Rappaport, *Cowards Don't Make History*.

9 More than half of UC Riverside's enrolled students are the first generation in their families to attend college. UC Riverside Institutional Research, "Enrollments: Demographic."

10 Enriquez et al., *Entre Familia*.

11 Nieves, *No Health Care? No Problem!*

12 Raza et al., "Interrupting the Cycle of Worrying."

13 In June 2012, John Morton, the director of Immigration and Customs Enforcement, issued a memo to all ICE employees to use prosecutorial discretion and avoid detention and deportation of young immigrants, students, those enlisted in the armed forces, those without criminal records, and those migrants who did not pose a threat to public safety. Immigrant rights activists subsequently questioned whether ICE agents followed the memo's directive, noting the detention and deportation of undocumented migrants without criminal records during the remainder of the Obama administration. When Donald Trump took office in 2017, the Morton memos were no longer regarded as guiding immigration enforcement. Morton, "Secretary Napolitano's Memorandum concerning the Exercise of Prosecutorial Discretion for Certain Removable Individuals Who Entered the United States as a Child," June 15, 2012, https://www.ice.gov/doclib/about/offices/ero/pdf/s1-certain-young-people-morton.pdf.

The "Undocumented and Unafraid" movement emerged after 2011, signaling that undocumented youth activists were no longer trying to apologize for family migration. On the contrary, they challenged what they perceived to be unjust immigration laws that allowed for the exploitation of immigrant labor but refused to grant civil rights. For more on this political history, including shifts in political ideology and political strategies, see Ábrego and Negrón-Gonzales, *We Are Not Dreamers*; Nicholls, *The DREAMers*.

14 Yosso, *Critical Race Counterstories along the Chicana, Chicano Educational Pipeline*, 43.

15 For an excellent social history of Self Help Graphics, including its deep connections to community and related political issues, see Reinoza and Davalos, *Self Help Graphics at Fifty*.

16 Epstein, "NCLR Head"; Krogstad, "DACA Has Shielded Nearly 790,000 Young Unauthorized Immigrants from Deportation."

17 During her time as a summer intern at UCLA's Labor Center, Jazmin learned that she was eligible to apply for DACA.

18 Latina Feminist Group, *Telling to Live*; Sommer, "Not Just a Personal Story."

19 Negrón-Gonzales, "Undocumented, Unafraid and Unapologetic," 272.
20 Nájera "Unauthorized Education."
21 Chavez, *The Latino Threat.*
22 For a vivid historical example, see Salinas, *Managed Migrations.*
23 Muñoz, *Identity, Social Activism, and the Pursuit of Higher Education,* 63.

Chapter 5. Mobilizing Undocumented Education

1 In her qualitative study with undocumented college students, Susana Muñoz noted that many activist students understood their access to higher education and their activist networks as a form of "capital." Muñoz, *Identity, Social Activism, and the Pursuit of Higher Education.*
2 Special thanks to Vanessa Fonseca-Chávez for help translating the lyrics.
3 Freire, *Pedagogy of the Oppressed,* 79.
4 In their pathbreaking article, Cecilia Menjívar and Leisy Ábrego draw from theories of structural and symbolic violence to theorize "legal violence," a type of violence that immigrants experience based on the impact the law on their lives. See Menjívar and Ábrego, "Legal Violence."
5 *Washington Post,* "Donald Trump Announces a Presidential Bid."
6 Despite this statewide policy that was supposed to limit cooperation between local law enforcement and ICE, certain counties refused to comply. A report by the ACLU found that sheriffs in several counties in California's Central Valley were cooperating directly with ICE. See Romani, "Collusion in California's Central Valley."
7 Nájera, "Creating Safe Space for Undocumented Students."
8 A growing literature examines the mental health of undocumented students. Sharon Velarde Pierce and her colleagues examine how legal vulnerability—a concept that helps explain the impact of individual or family immigration status on experiences of discrimination, social exclusion, economic insecurity, and threat of deportation or family separation—affects students' mental health. Velarde Pierce et al., "Evaluating the Effect of Legal Vulnerabilities and Social Support on the Mental Health of Undocumented College Students."
9 The University of California Immigrant Legal Services Center serves the immigration-related legal needs of UC immigrant students and their families.
10 Former president George W. Bush began a similar initiative with the Secure Fence Act of 2006. See Office of the Press Secretary, "Fact Sheet."
11 Executive Office of the President, "Enhancing Public Safety in the Interior of the United States"; Diamond, "Trump Orders Construction of Border Wall, Boosts Deportation Force."
12 Executive Office of the President, "Border Security and Immigration Enforcement Improvements."

13   Executive Office of the President, "Protecting the Nation from Foreign Terrorist Entry into the United States."

14   Bromwich. "Lawyers Mobilize at Nation's Airports after Trump's Order."

15   Ismail, "Protesters Occupy Bell Tower."

16   Escudero, *Organizing While Undocumented.*

17   Thrush, "Trump's New Travel Ban Blocks Migrants from Six Nations, Sparing Iraq." A. Naomi Paik provides a compelling analysis of the historical precedents of immigration bans and anti-Muslim federal policies that made the Trump ban legally sustainable. See Paik, *Bans, Walls, Raids, Sanctuary.*

18   Pearce and Lee, "Federal Immigration Agents Arrest a DACA-Eligible 'Dreamer' near Seattle, Lawsuit Says."

Ábrego, Leisy J. "Legal Consciousness of Undocumented Latinos: Fear and Stigma as Barriers to Claims-Making for First- and 1.5-Generation Immigrants." *Law and Society Review* 45, no. 2 (2011): 337–70. https://doi.org/10.1111/j.1540 -893.2011.00435.x.

Ábrego, Leisy J. *Sacrificing Families: Navigating Laws, Labor, and Love across Borders.* Stanford, CA: Stanford University Press, 2014.

Ábrego, Leisy J., and Genevieve Negrón-Gonzales, eds. *We Are Not Dreamers: Undocumented Scholars Theorize Undocumented Life in the United States.* Durham, NC: Duke University Press, 2020. https://doi.org/10.1515/9781478012382.

Alonso Bejarano, Carolina, Lucia López Juárez, Mirian A. Mijangos García, and Daniel M. Goldstein. *Decolonizing Ethnography: Undocumented Immigrants and New Directions in Social Science.* Durham, NC: Duke University Press, 2019. https://doi.org/10.1215/9781478004547.

Archibold, Randal C. "US Plans Border 'Surge' against Any Drug Wars." *New York Times,* January 7, 2009. https://www.nytimes.com/2009/01/08/us/08chertoff .html.

AVID. "What AVID Is: College and Career Readiness—Explore AVID Students by Grade Level." Accessed May 6, 2023. https://www.avid.org/what-avid-is.

Ayón, Cecilia, and David Becerra. "Mexican Immigrant Families under Siege: The Impact of Anti-immigrant Policies, Discrimination, and the Economic Crisis." *Advances in Social Work* 14, no. 1 (2013): 206–28. https://doi.org/10.18060/2692.

Ballotpedia. "Arizona SB 1070." Accessed January 24, 2022. https://ballotpedia.org /Arizona_SB_1070.

"Barry M. Goldwater Range-East." Arizona Department of Environmental Quality website. Accessed May 8, 2023. https://azdeq.gov/DOD/barry-m-goldwater-range.

Behar, Ruth, and Deborah A. Gordon, eds. *Women Writing Culture*. Berkeley: University of California Press, 1995.

Bernal, Dolores Delgado. "Learning and Living Pedagogies of the Home: The Mestiza Consciousness of Chicana Students." *International Journal of Qualitative Studies in Education* 14, no. 5 (September 1, 2001): 623–39. https://doi.org/10.1080/09518390110059838.

Bromwich, Jonah Engel. "Lawyers Mobilize at Nation's Airports after Trump's Order." *New York Times*, January 29, 2017. https://www.nytimes.com/2017/01/29/us/lawyers-trump-muslim-ban-immigration.html.

Cabrera, Gabrielle. "Disrupting Diversity: Undocumented Students in the Neoliberal University." In *We Are Not Dreamers*, edited by Leisy J. Ábrego and Genevieve Negrón-Gonzales, 66–86. Durham, NC: Duke University Press, 2020.

California Student Aid Commission. "About the California Student Aid Commission." February 1, 2018. https://www.csac.ca.gov/about.

Carpio, Genevieve. *Collisions at the Crossroads: How Place and Mobility Make Race*. American Crossroads, vol. 53. Berkeley: University of California Press, 2019.

Carpio, Genevieve, Clara Irazábal, and Laura Pulido. "Right to the Suburb? Rethinking Lefebvre and Immigrant Activism." *Journal of Urban Affairs* 33, no. 2 (2011): 185–208. https://doi.org/10.1111/j.1467-9906.2010.00535.x.

Chavez, Leo. *The Latino Threat: Constructing Immigrants, Citizens, and the Nation*. 2d ed. Redwood City, CA: Stanford University Press, 2013.

Chávez, Xóchitl. "'La Sierra Juárez en Riverside': The Inaugural Oaxacan Philharmonic Bands Audition on a University Campus." In *Theorizing Folklore from the Margins: Critical and Ethical Approaches*, edited by Solimar Otero and Mintzi Auanda Martínez-Rivera, 274–92. Bloomington: Indiana University Press, 2021.

City News Service. "Riverside Border Patrol Office to Close; Impact on Region Unclear." *Patch* (Murrieta, CA), July 12, 2012. https://patch.com/california/murrieta/riverside-border-patrol-office-to-close-impact-on-ill55dc920027.

Coalition for Humane Immigrant Rights. "Mission and History." Accessed August 16, 2021. https://www.chirla.org/who-we-are/about-us/mission-history.

Cornelius, Wayne A. "Death at the Border: Efficacy and Unintended Consequences of US Immigration Control Policy." *Population and Development Review* 27, no. 4 (2001): 661–85. https://doi.org/10.1111/j.1728-4457.2001.00661.x.

Corona, Rosalie, Lillian F. Stevens, Raquel W. Halfond, et al. "A Qualitative Analysis of What Latino Parents and Adolescents Think and Feel about Language Brokering." *Journal of Child and Family Studies* 21, no. 5 (2012): 788–98. https://doi.org/10.1007/s10826-011-9536-2.

Cruz, Adrian. "The Union within the Union: Filipinos, Mexicans and the Racial Integration of the Farm Worker Movement." *Social Movement Studies* 15, no. 4 (2016): 361–73.

De Genova, Nicholas. "Migrant 'Illegality' and Deportability in Everyday Life." *Annual Review of Anthropology* 31 (2002): 419–47.

De Lara, Juan. *Inland Shift: Race, Space, and Capital in Southern California.* Berkeley: University of California Press, 2018.

De Leon, Jason. *The Land of Open Graves: Living and Dying on the Migrant Trail.* California Series in Public Anthropology, vol. 36. Berkeley: University of California Press, 2015. https://doi.org/10.1525/9780520958685.

Diamond, Jeremy. "Trump Orders Construction of Border Wall, Boosts Deportation Force." CNN Politics, January 25, 2017. https://www.cnn.com/2017/01/25/politics/donald-trump-build-wall-immigration-executive-orders/index.html.

Durand, Jorge, and Douglas S. Massey. "The Costs of Contradiction: US Border Policy, 1986–2000." *Latino Studies* 1, no. 2 (2003): 233–52.

Engel, Patricia. *Infinite Country.* New York: Simon and Schuster, 2021.

Enriquez, Laura E. "'Because We Feel the Pressure and We Also Feel the Support': Examining the Educational Success of Undocumented Immigrant Latina/o Students." *Harvard Educational Review* 81, no. 3 (2011): 476–500. https://doi.org/10.17763/haer.81.3.w7k703q050143762.

Enriquez, Laura E. *Of Love and Papers: How Immigration Policy Affects Romance and Family.* Berkeley: University of California Press, 2020. https://directory.doabooks.org/handle/20.500.12854/32360.

Enriquez, Laura E., Cecilia Ayón, Basia D. Ellis, et al. "Persisting Inequalities and Paths Forward: A Report on the State of Undocumented Students in California's Public Universities." University of California Collaborative to Promote Immigrant and Student Equity, Irvine, December 2020. https://csu-csus.esploro.exlibrisgroup.com/esploro/outputs/99257874579901671?skipUsageReporting=true.

Enriquez, Laura E., Cecilia Ayón, Jennifer Nájera, et al. "Advancing Equity for Undocumented Students and Students from Mixed-Status Families at the University of California." University of California Collaborative to Promote Immigrant and Student Equity, Irvine, January 2021. https://ucpromise.uci.edu/reports/undocumented-and-mixed-status-families.

Enriquez, Laura E., Cecilia Ayón, Jennifer Nájera, et al. *Entre Familia* (forthcoming).

Enriquez, Laura E., Martha Morales Hernandez, Daniel Millán, and Daisy Vazquez Vera. "Mediating Illegality: Federal, State, and Institutional Policies in the Educational Experiences of Undocumented College Students." *Law and Social Inquiry* 44, no. 3 (2019): 679–703. https://doi.org/10.1017/lsi.2018.16.

Epstein, Reid J. "NCLR Head: Obama 'Deporter-in-Chief.'" *Politico*, March 4, 2014. https://www.politico.com/story/2014/03/national-council-of-la-raza-janet-murguia-barack-obama-deporter-in-chief-immigration-104217.

Escudero, Kevin. *Organizing While Undocumented: Immigrant Youth's Political Activism under the Law*, vol. 4. New York: New York University Press, 2020. https://doi.org/10.18574/nyu/9781479803194.001.0001

Estrada, Natalya. "Growing Up in San Bernardino: A Remembrance." KQED, December 20, 2015. https://www.kqed.org/news/10781988/growing-up-in-san-bernardino-a-remembrance.

Executive Office of the President. "Border Security and Immigration Enforcement Improvements." Executive Order (EO) 13767, January 25, 2017. *Federal Register*, January 30, 2017. https://www.federalregister.gov/documents/2017/01/30/2017–02095/border-security-and-immigration-enforcement-improvements.

Executive Office of the President. "Enhancing Public Safety in the Interior of the United States." Executive Order (EO) 13768, January 25, 2017. *Federal Register*, January 30, 2017. https://www.federalregister.gov/documents/2017/01/30/2017–02102/enhancing-public-safety-in-the-interior-of-the-united-states.

Executive Office of the President. "Protecting the Nation from Foreign Terrorist Entry into the United States." Executive Order (EO) 13769, January 27, 2017. *Federal Register*, February 1, 2017. https://www.federalregister.gov/documents/2017/02/01/2017–02281/protecting-the-nation-from-foreign-terrorist-entry-into-the-united-states.

Farfán-Santos, Elizabeth. *Undocumented Motherhood: Conversations on Love, Trauma, and Border Crossing*. Austin: University of Texas Press, 2022. https://doi.org/10.7560/326121.

Flores, Stella M. "State Dream Acts: The Effect of In-state Resident Tuition Policies and Undocumented Latino Students." *Review of Higher Education* 33, no. 2 (2010): 239–83. https://doi.org/10.1353/rhe.0.0134.

Freire, Paulo. *Pedagogy of the Oppressed: 30th Anniversary Edition*. Translated by Myra Bergman Ramos. London: Continuum, 2000.

Garcia, Matt. "Cesar Chavez and the United Farm Workers Movement." In *Oxford Research Encyclopedia of American History*, May 9, 2016. https://doi.org/10.1093/acrefore/9780199329175.013.217.

Garcia, Matthew. "Labor, Migration, and Social Justice in the Age of the Grape Boycott." *Gastronomica* 7, no. 3 (2007): 68–74. https://doi.org/10.1525/gfc.2007.7.3.68.

Geertz, Clifford. *The Interpretation of Cultures: Selected Essays*. New York: Basic, 1973.

Gonzales, Alfonso. *Reform without Justice: Latino Migrant Politics and the Homeland Security State*. New York: Oxford University Press, 2013. https://doi.org/10.1093/acprof:oso/9780199973392.001.0001.

Gonzales, Roberto G. "Learning to Be Illegal: Undocumented Youth and Shifting Legal Contexts in the Transition to Adulthood." *American Sociological Review* 76, no. 4 (2011): 602–19. https://doi.org/10.1177/0003122411411901.

Gonzales, Roberto G. *Lives in Limbo: Undocumented and Coming of Age in America*. Berkeley: University of California Press, 2015.

Gordon, Larry. "Napolitano Commits Funds to Aid UC Students Who Entered US Illegally." *Los Angeles Times*, October 30, 2013. https://www.latimes.com/nation/la-xpm-2013-oct-30-la-me-uc-napolitano-20131031-story.html.

Hale, Charles R. "What Is Activist Research?" *ITEMS Social Science Research Council* 2, nos. 1–2 (2001): 13–15.

HoSang, Daniel Martinez. *Racial Propositions: Ballot Initiatives and the Making of Postwar California.* American Crossroads 30. Berkeley: University of California Press, 2010. https://doi.org/10.1525/9780520947719.

"IGETC: What's IGETC?" University of California Admissions website. Accessed May 20, 2023. https://admission.universityofcalifornia.edu/admission -requirements/transfer-requirements/preparing-to-transfer/general-education -igetc/igetc.

Inda, Jonathan Xavier. *Targeting Immigrants: Government, Technology, and Ethics.* Malden, MA: Blackwell, 2006. https://doi.org/10.1002/9780470776315.

"Institutional Research and Academic Planning: California Master Plan for Higher Education." Office of the President, University of California. Accessed May 20, 2023. https://www.ucop.edu/institutional-research-academic-planning /content-analysis/academic-planning/california-master-plan.html.

Ismail, Evan. "Protesters Occupy Bell Tower; Show Statement against Trump's Immigration Policy." *The Highlander*, February 6, 2017. https://www .highlandernews.org/27559/protesters-occupy-bell-tower-show-statement -trumps-immigration-policy.

Krogstad, Jens Manuel. "DACA Has Shielded Nearly 790,000 Young Unauthorized Immigrants from Deportation." Pew Research Center, September 1, 2017. https://www.pewresearch.org/short-reads/2017/09/01/unauthorized -immigrants-covered-by-daca-face-uncertain-future.

Krogstad, Jens Manuel, Jeffrey S. Passel, and D'vera Cohn. "Five Facts about Illegal Immigration in the US." Pew Research Center, June 12, 2019. https://www.pew research.org/short-reads/2019/06/12/5-facts-about-illegal-immigration-in-the-u-s.

Kulish, Nicholas. "What It Costs to Be Smuggled across the US Border." *New York Times*, June 30, 2018. https://www.nytimes.com/interactive/2018/06/30/world /smuggling-illegal-immigration-costs.html.

Latina Feminist Group. *Telling to Live: Latina Feminist Testimonios.* Edited by Luz del Alba Acevedo, Norma Alarcón, Celia Alvarez, et al. Latin America Otherwise: Languages, Empires, Nations. Durham, NC: Duke University Press, 2001.

Lavín, Carlos E., and Grace L. Francis. "Looking in the Shadows: Literature on Undocumented Latinx Students with Disabilities." *Journal of Latinos and Education* (November 28, 2022): 424–37. https://doi.org/10.1080/15348431.2022.2149529.

Martinez, Daniel, Robin Reineke, Geoffrey Boyce, et al. "Migrant Deaths in Southern Arizona: Recovered Undocumented Border Crosser Remains Investigated by the Pima County Office of the Medical Examiner, 1990–2020." Social Science Research Network (SSRN) Scholarly Paper, April 21, 2021. https://papers .ssrn.com/abstract=3832193.

Massey, Douglas S. "Immigration Policy Mismatches and Counterproductive Outcomes: Unauthorized Migration to the US in Two Eras." *Comparative Migration Studies* 8, no. 1 (2020): 1–27. https://doi.org/10.1186/s40878-020-00181-6.

Maxson, Cheryl L., Karen Hennigan, David Sloane, and Kathy A. Kolnick. "Can Civil Gang Injunctions Change Communities? A Community Assessment of the Impact of Civil Gang Injunctions." Office of Justice Programs website, April 2004. https://www.ojp.gov/ncjrs/virtual-library/abstracts/can-civil-gang-injunctions-change-communities-community-assessment.

Menjívar, Cecilia, and Leisy J. Ábrego. "Legal Violence: Immigration Law and the Lives of Central American Immigrants." *American Journal of Sociology* 117, no. 5 (2012): 1380–421. https://doi.org/10.1086/663575.

Minian, Ana Raquel. *Undocumented Lives: The Untold Story of Mexican Migration*. Cambridge, MA: Harvard University Press, 2018. https://doi.org/10.4159/9780674919969.

Muñoz, Susana M. *Identity, Social Activism, and the Pursuit of Higher Education: The Journey Stories of Undocumented and Unafraid Community Activists*. Critical Studies of Latinxs in the Americas, vol. 4. New York: Peter Lang, 2015. https://www.peterlang.com/document/1118272.

Nájera, Jennifer R. *The Borderlands of Race: Mexican Segregation in a South Texas Town*. Washington, DC: University of Texas Press, 2015. https://doi.org/10.7560/767553.

Nájera, Jennifer R. "Creating Safe Space for Undocumented Students: Building on Politically Unstable Ground." *Anthropology and Education Quarterly* 51, no. 3 (2020): 341–58. https://doi.org/10.1111/aeq.12339.

Nájera, Jennifer R. "Remembering Migrant Life: Family Collective Memory and Critical Consciousness in the Midcentury Migrant Stream." *Oral History Review* 45, no. 2 (2018): 211–31. https://doi.org/10.1093/ohr/ohy037.

Nájera, Jennifer R. "Unauthorized Education: Challenging Borders between Good and Bad Immigrants." *Association of Mexican American Educators Journal* 9, no. 3 (August 1, 2015): 35–46.

Negrón-Gonzales, Genevieve. "Constrained Inclusion: Access and Persistence among Undocumented Community College Students in California's Central Valley." *Journal of Hispanic Higher Education* 16, no. 2 (2017): 105–22. https://doi.org/10.1177/1538192717697753.

Negrón-Gonzales, Genevieve. "Undocumented, Unafraid and Unapologetic: Re-articulatory Practices and Migrant Youth 'illegality.'" *Latino Studies* 12, no. 2 (2014): 259–78. https://doi.org/10.1057/lst.2014.20.

Negrón-Gonzales, Genevieve. "Undocumented Youth Activism as Counterspectacle: Civil Disobedience and Testimonio in the Battle around Immigration Reform." *Aztlán: A Journal of Chicano Studies* 40, no. 1 (March 15, 2015): 87–112.

Negrón-Gonzales, Genevieve, Leisy Ábrego, and Kathleen Coll. "Introduction: Immigrant Latina/o Youth and Illegality: Challenging the Politics of Deservingness." *Association of Mexican American Educators Journal* 9, no. 3 (2015): 7–10.

Ngai, Mae M. *Impossible Subjects: Illegal Aliens and the Making of Modern Amer-*

ica. Updated ed. Princeton, NJ: Princeton University Press, 2014. https://doi
.org/10.1515/9781400850235.

Nicholls, Walter J. *The DREAMers: How the Undocumented Youth Movement
Transformed the Immigrant Rights Debate*. Stanford, CA: Stanford University
Press, 2013.

Nieves, Marcos, dir. *No Health Care? No Problem!* UCLA Labor Center. April 22,
2014. YouTube video, 1:55. https://www.youtube.com/watch?v=RsD3Okvx
CMc.

Nuñez-Janes, Mariela, and Mario Ovalle. "Organic Activists: Undocumented
Youth Creating Spaces of Acompañamiento." *Diaspora, Indigenous, and Minority Education* 10, no. 4 (2016): 189–200.

Office of the Press Secretary. "Fact Sheet: The Secure Fence Act of 2006."
Press release, White House Archive, President George W. Bush, October
26, 2006. https://georgewbush-whitehouse.archives.gov/news/releases
/2006/10/20061026-1.html.

Olivares, Mariela. "Renewing the Dream: DREAM Act Redux and Immigration
Reform." *Harvard Latino Law Review* 16 (2013): 79–125.

Paik, A. Naomi. *Bans, Walls, Raids, Sanctuary: Understanding U. S. Immigration
for the Twenty-First Century*. American Studies Now: Critical Histories of the
Present, vol. 12. Berkeley: University of California Press, 2020.

Passel, Jeffrey S., D'vera Cohn, and Ana Gonzalez Barrera. "Net Migration
from Mexico Falls to Zero—and Perhaps Less." Pew Research Center, April
23, 2012. https://www.pewresearch.org/race-and-ethnicity/2012/04/23/net
-migration-from-mexico-falls-to-zero-and-perhaps-less.

Pearce, Matt, and Kurtis Lee. "Federal Immigration Agents Arrest a DACA-Eligible
'Dreamer' near Seattle, Lawsuit Says." *Los Angeles Times*, February 14, 2017.
https://www.latimes.com/nation/la-na-ice-daca-20170214-story.html.

Pérez, William. *Americans by Heart: Undocumented Latino Students and the Promise of Higher Education*. Multicultural Education Series. New York: Teachers
College Press, 2012.

Ramirez Resendiz, Chantiri. "Subjectivity Making in Undocumented Student Organizing." PhD diss., University of California, Los Angeles, 2016.

Rappaport, Joanne. *Cowards Don't Make History: Orlando Fals Borda and the Or-
igins of Participatory Action Research*. Durham, NC: Duke University Press,
2020. https://doi.org/10.1215/9781478012542.

Raza, Syeda S., Zyshia Williams, Dalal Katsiaficas, and Lydia A. Saravia. "Interrupting the Cycle of Worrying: Financial Implications of the California DREAM Act
in the Lives of Undocumented College Students." *Review of Higher Education*
43, no. 1 (2019): 335–70. https://doi.org/10.1353/rhe.2019.0098.

Reinoza, Tatiana, and Karen Mary Davalos, eds. *Self Help Graphics at Fifty: A Cor-
nerstone of Latinx Art and Collaborative Artmaking*. Berkeley, CA: University
of California Press, 2023.

Rendón, Laura I. "Community College Puente: A Validating Model of Education." *Educational Policy* 16, no. 4 (2002): 642–67.

Richman, Josh. "Undocumented Students Disrupt Janet Napolitano's Speech at UC Summit." *Mercury News*, May 7, 2015. https://www.mercurynews.com/2015/05/07/undocumented-students-disrupt-janet-napolitanos-speech-at-uc-summit.

Romani, Maria. "Collusion in California's Central Valley: The Case for Ending Sheriff Entanglement with ICE." San Francisco: American Civil Liberties Union Foundation of Northern California, February 9, 2022. https://www.aclunc.org/sites/default/files/ICE_report_screen_0.pdf.

Rosaldo, Renato. *Culture and Truth: The Remaking of Social Analysis*. Boston: Beacon, 1993.

Rosales, William E., Laura E. Enriquez, and Jennifer R. Nájera. "Politically Excluded, Undocu-engaged: The Perceived Effect of Hostile Immigration Policies on Undocumented Student Political Engagement." *Journal of Latinos and Education* 20, no. 3 (2021): 260–75. https://doi.org/10.1080/15348431.2021.1949991.

Rosas, Gilberto. *Barrio Libre: Criminalizing States and Delinquent Refusals of the New Frontier*. Durham, NC: Duke University Press, 2012. https://doi.org/10.1515/9780822391838.

Rose, Joel. "Immigration Agencies Ordered Not to Use Term 'Illegal Alien' under New Biden Policy." National Public Radio, April 19, 2021. https://www.npr.org/2021/04/19/988789487/immigration-agencies-ordered-not-to-use-term-illegal-alien-under-new-biden-polic.

Sahagun, Louis. "LA Gangs, Drugs Invade Inland Empire." *Los Angeles Times*, August 11, 1988. https://www.latimes.com/archives/la-xpm-1988-08-11-mn-391-story.html.

Salinas, Cristina. *Managed Migrations: Growers, Farmworkers, and Border Enforcement in the Twentieth Century*. Historia USA. Austin: University of Texas Press, 2018. https://doi.org/10.7560/316146.

Santa-Ramirez, Stephen. "A Sense of Belonging: The People and Counterspaces Latinx Undocu/DACAmented Collegians Use to Persist." *Education Sciences* 12, no. 10 (2022): 691. https://doi.org/10.3390/educsci12100691.

Seif, Hinda. "'Unapologetic and Unafraid': Immigrant Youth Come Out from the Shadows." Edited by Constance A. Flanagan and Brian D. Christens. *New Directions for Child and Adolescent Development*, no. 134 (2011): 59–75. https://doi.org/10.1002/cd.311.

Sepúlveda, Enrique, III. "Toward a Pedagogy of Acompañamiento: Mexican Migrant Youth Writing from the Underside of Modernity." *Harvard Educational Review* 81, no. 3 (2011): 550–73. https://doi.org/10.17763/haer.81.3.088mv5t704828u67.

Sleeter, Christine E. "The Academic and Social Value of Ethnic Studies: A Research Review." Report, National Education Association Research Department, Washington, DC, 2011. https://eric.ed.gov/?id=ED521869.

Smith, Linda Tuhiwai. *Decolonizing Methodologies: Research and Indigenous Peoples*. London: Zed, 1999.

Solórzano, Daniel, Miguel Ceja, and Tara Yosso. "Critical Race Theory, Racial Microaggressions, and Campus Racial Climate: The Experiences of African American College Students." *Journal of Negro Education* 69, nos. 1–2 (Winter 2000): 60–73.

Sommer, Doris. "'Not Just a Personal Story': Women's Testimonios and the Plural Self." In *Life/Lines: Theorizing Women's Autobiography*, edited by Bella Brodzki and Celeste Schenck, 107–30. Ithaca, NY: Cornell University Press, 2019. https://doi.org/10.7591/9781501745560-008.

Soto, Lilia. *Girlhood in the Borderlands: Mexican Teens Caught in the Crossroads of Migration*, vol. 1. New York: New York University Press, 2018. https://doi.org/10.18574/nyu/9781479888399.001.0001.

Speed, Shannon. "At the Crossroads of Human Rights and Anthropology: Toward a Critically Engaged Activist Research." *American Anthropologist* 108, no. 1 (2006): 66–76. https://doi.org/10.1525/aa.2006.108.1.66.

Suárez-Orozco, Marcelo, Robert T. Teranishi, and Carola Suárez-Orozco. "In the Shadows of the Ivory Tower: Undocumented Undergraduates and the Liminal State of Immigration Reform." UCLA (2015). https://escholarship.org/uc/item/2hq679z4.

Thrush, Glenn. "Trump's New Travel Ban Blocks Migrants from Six Nations, Sparing Iraq." *New York Times*, March 6, 2017. https://www.nytimes.com/2017/03/06/us/politics/travel-ban-muslim-trump.html.

Truax, Eileen. *How Does It Feel to Be Unwanted? Stories of Resistance and Resilience from Mexicans Living in the United States*. Translated by Diane Stockwell. Boston: Beacon, 2018.

UC Riverside Institutional Research. "Enrollments: Demographic." Accessed May 26, 2023. https://ir.ucr.edu/stats/enroll/demographic.

Urrea, Luis Alberto. *The Devil's Highway: A True Story*. New York: Little, Brown, 2004.

Valdés, Guadalupe, Christina Chávez, and Claudia Angelelli. "A Performance Team: Young Interpreters and Their Parents." In *Expanding Definitions of Giftedness*, 63–98. New York: Routledge, 2003. https://doi.org/10.4324/9781410607249-3.

Vazquez Vera, Daisy, M. Liliana Ramirez, and Laura E. Enriquez. *Struggling: Undocumented Students' Financial Need*. Irvine, CA: The Undocumented Student Equity Project, December 2018. https://static1.squarespace.com/static/5aea8933372b96f1537d0178/t/5c101ae4562fa7b47c40726e/1544559335578/Struggling-VazquezVera+et+al+2018.pdf.

Velarde Pierce, Sharon, Alein Y. Haro, Cecilia Ayón, and Laura E. Enriquez. "Evaluating the Effect of Legal Vulnerabilities and Social Support on the Mental Health of Undocumented College Students." *Journal of Latinos and Education* 20, no. 3 (2021): 246–59. https://doi.org/10.1080/15348431.2021.1949990.

Visweswaran, Kamala. *Fictions of Feminist Ethnography*. Minneapolis: University of Minnesota Press, 1994.

Washington Post. "Donald Trump Announces a Presidential Bid." June 16, 2015. https://colorustrumped.com/wp-content/uploads/notation-trumps-candidacy-announcement.pdf.

Yosso, Tara J. *Critical Race Counterstories along the Chicana, Chicano Educational Pipeline*. Teaching/Learning Social Justice Series. New York: Routledge, 2005. https://doi.org/10.4324/9780203624821.

Zavella, Patricia. *I'm Neither Here nor There: Mexicans' Quotidian Struggles with Migration and Poverty*. Durham, NC: Duke University Press, 2011. https://doi.org/10.1515/9780822394259.

tion and, 67; of student activists, 140; undocumented education and, 11, 125; among undocumented students, 64, 125, 140

community cultural wealth, 8, 43–44

Conoley, Jane Close, 89–90

consciousness: class, 44; critical, 44, 61, 65, 94; legal, 8, 67, 85, 93–94; pedagogies of home and, 44; political, 8, 13, 66–68, 71, 76, 85, 93–94, 99, 104–5, 116, 135

Cornelius, Wayne, 24

coyotes (smugglers), 24, 39–40

criminalization: of reentry, 23–24; of undocumented migrants, 21, 23–24, 57, 123, 129; of undocumented parents, 7; of undocumented students, 111

DACA (Deferred Action for Childhood Arrivals), 9, 12, 99; application, 53; deportation reprieve, 113–14; deservingness and, 19, 123; driver's licenses and, 54; eligibility, 19, 47, 48–49, 53, 114, 156n17; markers of adulthood and, 149n35; PODER workshops on, 110–11; privileges of, 120, 123, 138; Trump attempt to terminate, 10, 124, 130; work permits, 36, 47, 88, 111, 114, 142

Davis, Gray, 82

DeGenova, Nicholas, 20

deportation, 3; DACA reprieve, 68; under Immigration and Nationality Act, 132; mental health and, 129; Morton memos, 110, 156n13; under Obama, 113–14, 156n13; 2016 presidential election and, 14

deservingness: citizenship and, 19–20, 38, 83; class and, 20; of Dreamers, 20; of immigrants, 10, 19–20; politics of, 8; of undocumented parents, 10, 19–20, 154n34; of undocumented students, 19–20

detention: border militarization and, 149n21; under Immigration and Nationality Act, 132; immigra-

tion policy and, 108, 132; Morton memos, 110, 156n13; under Obama, 113–14, 156n13

detention centers: immigration laws and, 108; Los Angeles Metropolitan Detention Center, 118, 121–22

diversity, 139, 153n15; as capital, 7; Napolitano statement on, 126–27

DREAM (Development, Relief, and Education for Alien Minors) Act, 20, 38, 150n40; advocacy for, 83; citizenship and, 21, 31, 38, 68, 86, 154n33; failure to pass, 31, 68, 86, 88, 154n33. *See also* California Development, Relief, and Education for Alien Minors (DREAM) Act

Dreamer discourse, 20–21; immigration reform and, 20, 148n7; parents and, 83, 148n10

Dreamers, 19, 31; deservingness of, 20; fallacy of, 7; "undeserving" parents and, 10, 20

Dreaming of Higher Education conference, 104–9, 105 fig. 4.1; California DREAM Act workshops, 110–11; community education, 111; teaching of educational staff, 111

education, 8; activism and, 6, 10, 13, 14; assimilation and, 66; community building and, 67; immigration policy and, 86; pedagogies of home and, 42–44; political, 65, 67; problem-posing, 76; tracking, 150n3; of undocumented students, 6–7, 86. *See also* undocumented education

English Language Learner programs, 26

Enriquez, Laura, 21, 151n13

Escudero, Kevin, 98, 135

ethnic studies, 8, 76, 154n21; Chicanx studies, 3, 8, 12

ethnography, 12. *See also* anthropology

farmwork, 44–46; youth labor, 151n10

farmworkers, 92–93; Border Patrol and, 20; UFW, 45, 80, 128

tarization and, 19; of undocumented students, 6–7, 19

Trump, Donald, 99; anti-immigrant platform and policies, 114, 124–26, 129–32, 133 fig. 5.2, 156n13; anti-Muslim policies, 124, 125, 132–35, 133 fig. 5.2, 158n17

UCLA Labor Center, 108
UC Office of the President (UCOP), 3–4
UC Undocumented Student Coalition, 38, 60, 139, 140, 150n43
UC Undocumented Student Summit, 3–6, 37; Chant Down the Walls march, 118–24; protest of Napolitano, 3, 4 fig. I.1, 5–6, 7, 14–15, 15 fig. I.2, 37, 60, 97
UER (La Unión Estudiantil de la Raza), 28–29, 30–31, 76, 94, 106; organizational support, 104, 110; political consciousness and, 85; unity building and, 69–71
UFW (United Farm Workers of America), 45, 80, 128
Undocumented and Unafraid movement, 110, 121, 140, 156n13
undocumented education, 7–8; circulation of knowledge, 124–25; community building and, 11, 125; community education and, 97–98; informal sites of, 65, 94; lived experience and, 19; pedagogies of home, 139; PODER and, 66, 124–25, 139; political organizations and, 7; student organizations and, 7, 65, 95. *See also* education
undocumented parents: activism and, 117; advocacy of, 56–57, 59; belonging of, 103; criminalization of, 129; deservingness of, 10, 19–20, 154n34; Dreamer discourse and, 20, 83, 148n10; work ethics of, 49
undocumented people: advocacy for, 44; driver's licenses, 7, 51, 54, 84, 151n21; legal vulnerability and, 157n8; mobility of, 43, 60, 104, 151n7
undocumented student activists: ad-

vocacy work of, 97–99, 107, 140; capital of, 157n1; Chant Down the Walls march, 118–24, 119 fig. 5.1; community building and, 140; dissemination of information, 98; political consciousness and, 135; subjectivity of, 7; testimonio, use of, 114–17; Undocumented and Unafraid movement, 110, 156n13
undocumented students: as "AB 540," 64, 74, 79; anti-immigrant sentiment and, 90; belonging of, 26, 44, 48–49, 58, 93–94, 98, 151n14; civic engagement of, 65–66, 74–76, 152n4; community and, 107, 144–45; community building, 64, 125; criminalization of, 111; deservingness of, 19–20; with disabilities, 120, 152n31; driver's licenses for, 62–64, 70, 126; education of, 6–7; as educators, 37, 102–3; English learning, 41, 71, 140; financial aid for, 3, 27, 30, 36–37, 47, 48, 58–59, 64, 70, 74–75, 88–89, 102, 110, 126, 149n35, 151n13; financial struggles of, 16, 46, 48, 75, 77–79, 90–91, 92–93, 142, 144; inclusion of, 118–20; in-state tuition policies, 27, 64, 102, 116, 126, 152n2, 154n26, 155n6; institutional support for, 3, 84, 98, 104–7, 110–11, 130, 136, 157n9; mental health of, 129, 157n8; mentoring of, 46–47, 54; milestones of adulthood, 66, 74–75, 153n8; navigating "illegality," 79, 86, 139; as 1.5 generation, 66, 153n6; political consciousness of, 76, 85, 99, 104–5; political engagement of, 65–66, 152n5; school tracking and, 150n3; stigma and fear, 66–68, 71; stress and, 31, 66–67, 153n9
university, the: belonging and, 111; neoliberalism and, 7; political consciousness and, 67; positive campus racial climates, 153n15; safe spaces and, 71; undocumented education and, 8, 124